(continued from front flap) design; market research; personnel, placement and executive recruiting; photography; public relations and fund-raising; publishing (book, magazine, and newspaper) ; radio and television; real estate; telephone; and travel. She describes in detail the way each business works—how each department functions; what the job titles mean—and she gives the educational and personal qualities needed not only for the business as a whole but for each division of it. She includes as well the advancement possibilities; the areas in which job opportunities are most prevalent; and the salary range.

The book ends with two chapters for special kinds of job-seekers: the *Returner* (the woman going back to work after years off for child-raising) ; and the *Job-Changer* (the beginner who gets discouraged about the routine quality of her job; the woman who after years of work feels she has gone about as far as she can go in her present company).

Alice Gore King consulted with members of each field she covers in order to accumulate the most accurate and up-to-date information possible on how each job works and what the job-seeker can do to find a place in it. And she has put that information in a book so truly useful and yet so thoroughly readable that it will prove a delightful as well as essential guide for every woman looking for a business career.

CAREER
OPPORTUNITIES
FOR WOMEN
IN BUSINESS

CAREER
OPPORTUNITIES
FOR WOMEN
IN BUSINESS

BY ALICE GORE KING

1963

E. P. DUTTON & CO., INC. • NEW YORK

CONTENTS

I	WHY THIS BOOK	3
II	LOOKING FOR A JOB	7
III	CLERICAL AND SECRETARIAL	24
IV	NON-PROFESSIONAL JOBS WITHIN THE PROFESSIONS	32
V	ADVERTISING	40
VI	ARMED SERVICES	50
VII	AUTOMATION	57
VIII	BOOKKEEPING AND ACCOUNTING	64
IX	FASHION AND RETAILING	70
X	FINANCE	81
XI	FREE-LANCE	90
XII	GOVERNMENT	96
XIII	INSURANCE	105
XIV	INTERIOR DESIGN	114
XV	MARKET RESEARCH	119
XVI	PERSONNEL—PLACEMENT—EXECUTIVE RECRUITING	126
XVII	PHOTOGRAPHY	137
XVIII	PUBLIC RELATIONS AND FUND-RAISING	140

vi   *Contents*

xix	PUBLISHING	148
xx	RADIO AND TELEVISION	167
xxi	REAL ESTATE	176
xxii	TELEPHONE	179
xxiii	TRAVEL	182
xxiv	THE RETURNER	189
xxv	CHANGING JOBS	195
	PUBLICATIONS MENTIONED IN THIS BOOK	203
	ACKNOWLEDGMENTS	205
	INDEX	207

CAREER
OPPORTUNITIES
FOR WOMEN
IN BUSINESS

I

WHY THIS BOOK

The purpose of this book is to take a close look at what is actually involved in different jobs, to help you recognize the opportunities and fit yourself for your choice—and introduce you to the people, characteristics, demands of the business world. It is directed at the person looking for her first job after school or college, but the seasoned job holder or the returner can read it over her shoulder, since the same principles apply. Those who have not reached the job-hunting stage have a chance to do some thinking ahead.

Whether you work for bread and butter, for jam, or for fun, you should relate your education to your goals, find out all you can about the conditions of various jobs, and enjoy your work.

ABOUT EDUCATION. Sound decisions concerning education form a base for a successful career. In former days executives got to the top by hard work. Many of our current business and professional leaders never went beyond high school. They made sure, however, that their education did not stop there. The same thing can be done today, but progress can be faster and easier for those with college degrees.

If you go to college, though, be sure it is for the right reason, for success depends also on realistic thinking about the meaning of your degree.

A liberal arts education is background, ideal for whatever you pursue: a job (paid, volunteer, or keeping house), graduate school, travel, or just living. It is not vocational training, although it happens that those who major in science, mathematics, or statistics are vocationally prepared upon graduation. A liberal arts student should not feel hog-tied by her specialty. English majors do not have to go into publishing; French majors need not become interpreters. As a matter of fact, many UN translators regard language as a tool, not as a focus; they themselves have been drawn from the ranks of lawyers, economists, teachers.

An A.B. teaches you mental discipline, to meet new situations, use your initiative, follow directives as well as directions. That is why employers want college graduates. The degree is a sign of what you *can* do, not what you *have* done. But besides graduating, you must be able to do something specific the day you are hired. Your A.B. signifies a mind that knows what it can and cannot do, and the willingness to acquire whatever you need for your first job.

You may wonder why you should go to college if you can't rest on your sheepskin. An A.B. has been compared to a label on a trunk; it does not change the contents, but helps it reach its destination: college graduates earn 60 per cent more in a lifetime than do high school graduates.

The need for technical and professional people in our labor force is increasing more rapidly than for any other occupational group. Employers not only *can* demand a college education, but *must*.

High school graduates can get a toe hold in jobs where college is called for, and catch up on further education later. Employers are helping employees take courses by giving them time off and refunding part of the tuition. In any case, education never stops.

WHAT IS A JOB LIKE? Knowledge of job requirements and features is another cornerstone of your career decision.

Jobs may require that you deal with numbers or people or words; work with machines, your hands, your voice, or on your feet. Some have odd hours and shifts, are in noisy surroundings, make you a member of a team, pay low salaries, or have many benefits. Take these considerations into account as you learn about actual duties.

There will be surprises. Those of you who want to work with people and not figures can still find satisfaction in a bank; those who don't like to sell might nevertheless be happy in retailing; those who enjoy detailed paper work may find it in personnel; those who want to write need not confine themselves to a publication; those who want to be creative will discover there are no creative jobs, only creative people.

If you want to use *all* your talents, it is up to you to find ways to use them in your job. Someone hired as a secretary can find herself doing research for a bulletin, writing it, and designing the layout. If it is people you want, in what relationship? Do you want to direct them, as a lawyer, teacher, doctor; tend them, as a nurse or social worker; share the work with them, as a partner; follow their lead, as an assistant or right-hand man?

Physical attributes of jobs can be as important as mental. Chemists like the smell of acids and gases; sailors enjoy the stickiness of salt on the boom; stonecutters, oil painters, flute players select their medium partly on the basis of feel. Think of your sentiments about books, drafting boards, inky fingers, bright lights, factory noises, hard floors, sudden temperature changes. Be steered but not strapped by these emotional tones. Some people, proud of their brain power, allow themselves to be helpless with their hands. A little brain power applied to a mechanical task can make the hands more dexterous.

WORK CAN BE FUN. A hundred years ago women started going to college; forty years ago they went to the polls; today they go to work. Many things have changed in these hundred years. But today, as then, those who enjoy their work do the best jobs, and help all around them do *their* best jobs too.

People who don't enjoy their work show it through absenteeism, job hopping, or by not starting their work until nine o'clock even when they reach the office before then.

Yet most of the people who do enjoy their work had to learn to. Sometimes they made careful advance appraisals. Sometimes they learned by seeing people working who didn't have to. One woman exclaimed recently, "Look at the hobbyists who turn out professional products that draw high prices; the millionaires who seek and fill demanding government jobs; the retired men and women who continue to work by choice, not for cash."

WHEN READING THIS BOOK. Keep these points in mind. Jobs, duties, titles vary from one company to another and are not always as clear-cut as the descriptions here. And there are exceptions to some of the dogmatic statements, for admittedly people do get jobs by roads said to be blocked off:

Secretarial skills are the way into publishing, but Florence R went right from college onto a magazine, rose from clip girl to religious editor on the strength of her writing ability and wide knowledge, and is now education editor of a large newspaper. She has never set finger to typewriter.

Woman's place is in women's fields, not heavy industry. Yet one woman who has been in the news often, because of her refusal to withhold taxes from her employees' wages, was for years owner and manager of a profitable cable-grip business.

And you may have a friend who found the kind of job you would like and yet got it without following the rules.

This book gives details. Your job is to apply them to *yourself*.

II

LOOKING FOR A JOB

It used to be that looking for a job was a hat-in-hand process. Today it's a do-it-yourself one. It is selling a service, not looking for a job, whether the applicant is just starting out or changing one job for another. The principles of good job hunting are those of good sales technique.

Approach the job hunt from the angle of selling a product —which is you.

YOUR MARKET. When you are ready to look, and *know what you want,* find the channels that lead you to jobs. Your school or college counselors know where openings are, and have some listed in their files. Sign up for interviews with company recruiters who visit the campus. Your friends, relatives, and former employers should know of your job interests. Check the help-wanted advertisements in newspapers of the city where you are going to look. Register with State Employment Services and employment agencies. Some will accept your application before you graduate; others won't until you are ready to work. Tell them what you want, what you can do. Present your qualifications to them as you would to a prospective employer; they are influential in getting you hired. Fill out their applications fully and willingly; it is your first chance to show your work. Get in practice: you have many licenses, insurance forms, tax reports ahead of you in life. Read the form through first; complete it neatly and accurately; proofread it afterward.

See page 9 for the kind of items you will find on application blanks.

Commercial agencies charge a fee for getting you a job, and regulations vary with the state. Read the contract before you sign it to avoid misunderstandings. Think kindly of agencies. They may interview a hundred applicants before they place a dozen. The fees may seem high from your point of view, but add up slowly from theirs, and must pay for the substantial amount of work necessary to line up job openings for you.

Besides using these channels to jobs, compile your own list (from libraries) of companies for whom you would like to work, and go directly to them.

Take pencil and paper, the dates you may be asked for, references and their addresses, and a résumé to enable others to learn about you quickly. That requires homework.

KNOW YOURSELF.   One day a partition salesman tried to interest a customer in other items in his catalogue, but when asked the price of a typewriter, he didn't know; his field was partitions. If a salesman doesn't know his goods, he won't be able to sell them. So it is with what *you* have to sell.

To know yourself, analyze your experience, skills, aptitude, interests:

—your courses: what you majored in, did well in, liked best.
—extracurricular activities: school offices, committees, athletics.
—jobs you held during school and summers: don't be modest about these; employers *are* interested, not because of what you did, but because you did them.
—your skills: typing or shorthand speeds; office machines you operate—mimeograph, comptometer, dictaphone; languages you are fluent in.
—your abilities: are you good at math or better with words?

SAMPLE EMPLOYMENT APPLICATION FORM

Name_____Date_____
      (last)   (first)

Address_____Social Security No._____

_____Position desired_____

Home telephone_____Location desired_____

Business telephone_____Salary range_____

Birthdate_____ Age_____ Height___ Weight___ Physical defects?_____

Marital status_____ Dependents_____ U.S. citizen?_____

Will you accept work that is: Temporary___Part-time___Out-of-town___

Do you drive a car?_____ Own a car?_____ Other licenses_____

Will you accept collect telegrams and telephones?_____

EDUCATION	Name	Years Attended	Year Graduated	Major
High School				
College				
Business School				
Other				

LANGUAGES: Speak_____ Read_____ Write_____

SKILLS: Shorthand speed and system _____

       Typing speed___ PBX___ Monitor___ Bookkeeping___

       Office machines _____

EMPLOYMENT (list most recent job first)

Name & Address	Nature of Business	Your Job	Your Superior	Dates Held	Salary	Reason for Leaving

REFERENCES AND ADDRESSES (list three)_____

Quick to understand new concepts, or slow but solid once you have learned something? They are all assets but for different uses.

—your interests: you do best what you like best. Even if you master something you don't like, you may want to change to something else years later and it won't be easy then. Try to make the right choice at the beginning when you can make up for lack of training if necessary.

YOUR SALES STORY.   Boil down this analysis into a presentation of your qualities, abilities, experience, *plus* the accomplishments. Not merely a record of experience. Try not to settle for the kind of data sheet or chronological résumé which is merely a list of job titles, duties, addresses, unless you are in a professional field or are a beginner with no experience, or unless an employer or agency has asked for such a résumé. Describe your experience in terms of problems you have met, what you did about them, what the results were—create a functional résumé to get an interview. You will find as many opinions about résumé-writing as people you consult; there is no fixed answer. Make one that represents *you*.

For instance, don't just say:

In the summer of 1959, while secretary to the sales manager of the Dress Company, Newark, N.J., I acted as telephone-receptionist, typed routine correspondence, kept track of requests and complaints of customers.

Do show how you performed your job:

As telephone-receptionist at the Dress Company, Newark, N.J., in the summer of 1959, my job was to greet customers and take care of their requests and complaints while turning out routine correspondence between callers. I wrote down each complaint, told the person that he would get prompt attention, and saw that he did. Three of the several hundred visitors expressed appreciation to my boss.

Here are some examples of effective résumés:

June A
Collegiate College
Collegeville, Ohio

PUBLIC RELATIONS TRAINEE

Writing

Assistant in the college News Bureau during my junior and senior
years

    I wrote news releases about student activities (swimming awards,
scholarships, marriages) for home town newspapers all over the
country. One article was used in a journalism course as an example of packed writing.

Publicity Assistant for the Conference on Public Relations Today

    I attended panel discussions, abstracted printed speeches,
prepared releases, and arranged for radio interviews with
delegates to the conference. Before the end of the sessions,
I was asked to cover the meetings the following year.

Editing

As Editor in Chief of the campus newspaper -

    I wrote, headlined, edited, proofread news, feature and sports
stories, and made up page and advertising layout.

While Art Editor of the undergraduate magazine whose final issue
sold more copies than any in its history -

    I selected and redesigned cartoons, illustrations, and adver-
tisements.

Work with Groups

I was Orientation Leader of seniors for a six-week indoctrination
program for freshman, and Cheer Leader for two years. I also
selected and trained twenty assistants for the College News.

Memberships

Committee on Undergraduate Affairs
Student Government Association
Placement Office Board
International Relations Club

Skills

Typing: 65 wpm
Lettering, proofreading, newspaper make-up, magazine design

Education

Collegiate College, A.B. 1962. Major: English
   Thesis: "The Function of the Public Relations Office
           in a College"

May R (Mrs. J.W.)
111 East 1 Street
Los Ville, Calif.
444-9876

PRESS
INFORMATION

As a result of handling hundreds of press
releases about the theatre, I am consulted
not only by the general public but by radio
and TV broadcasters. Much of the material
used by the Blank Foundation in its docu-
mentary on the History of American Acting
came from my files.

PROMOTION

To promote good relations between store
employees and management, I originated a
news column about store personnel for their
house organ, interviewed sales clerks,
packers, buyers, and executives, and wrote
the finished copy. The employees felt themselves so much a part of the store that when
it ran into financial reverses they offered
to take a temporary wage cut.

EDITING

As editor of a technical publication, I
covered annual conventions and wrote up the
proceedings of meetings. For the monthly
magazine I rewrote engineers' articles to
fit the space, and translated technical
notes into lay terms.

NEWS

On a Paris newspaper during the war, I was
assistant to a foreign correspondent, did
the research on American news, and wrote
the stories. This paper was the first to
carry the news of the invention of plexi-
glass for bombers, and I was responsible
for that scoop.

CONTACT

Because of my interest in mass media, I
spend a good deal of free time in TV studios
and control booths, during rehearsals and
actual performances. Consequently, I meet
producers, directors, production men, and
technical assistants. This enables me to
fill in background quickly and accurately
when it is needed for news stories.

LANGUAGES

French, German, Italian

EDUCATION

United High School, 1935

EMPLOYERS

Publicity Associates, Inc., New York
Fashion Store, San Francisco
Institute of Technicians' Manuals, New York
Les Idées, Paris

Iris S
Eastern College
Easternberg, Md.

Résumé

PAID WORK EXPERIENCE

During college   Campus Representative for the Writing Paper Co.

I distributed samples of note paper to students and faculty, and made regular reports of sales and of suggestions about advertising. I received special praise for the fullness of my reports.

Summer 1958   Clerk in the Public Relations Department of Tennis Sportswear, Newton, Mass.

Did typing and filing of confirmations of customers' orders, and compiled the weekly sales reports. I filed over 4,000 pieces of materials, and responded to some 300 requisitions for data from these files. Only twice was I unable to find a requested letter.

EXTRA CURRICULAR   Freshman class vice president
Member of the dormitory library committee

EDUCATION   Eastern College, A.B. 1959
Major: Philosophy

SKILLS   Typing: 45
Shorthand: intend to learn

REFERENCES   On file with the Eastern College Office of Student Placement, Easternberg, Md.

GOOD PRESENTATION. Like the salesman's flyers, your résumé must be readable. Make use of white space, capitals, indentation, underlining. Remember as a child you preferred books with lots of conversation? That was partly because they had so much white space, instead of long paragraphs from margin to margin.

Notice: explain the titles you have had—a vice president in advertising and a college vice president have different assignments; list jobs first (this is meant to be a teaser; the employer will ask about your education and other background *after* he sees what you can *do*); include only the positive—the shoe-polish label doesn't say it can't shine silver; you don't say you speak Spanish poorly.

Two free forums in New York teach job hunters the technique of making résumés; the Job Finding Forum of the Advertising Club meets at 7:30 on Monday and Wednesday evenings at 103 East 35th Street; and the Man Marketing Clinic of the Sales Executives Club, Tuesdays at 7:00 P.M. at 51 Madison Avenue. Headquarters of these groups in other cities can tell you if they run forums there.

Do your own résumé; don't hire someone else to write one for you. The very process of remembering and organizing gives you self-confidence and equipment for interviews, and is one of the chief things to be gained from making a résumé.

Friends who offer to lend a hand in finding you a job should have copies of your résumé. An uncle may know only that he thinks you're wonderful. His enthusiasm can be made specific through the résumé. Ask him to introduce you to people who have jobs to offer, but don't try to use pull or bypass the personnel department if you are asked to go there first. You can get the job if you can fill it; influence won't help if you can't. Use your head in sizing up interviews with your uncle's friends. One girl was interviewed by a corporation president, and then when she got the job was disappointed to find herself in a big room full of clicking typewriters, not in a private office with leather chairs and personal telephones.

Artists and writers should have a portfolio of samples. Slip examples of your work into the transparent pages of a standard size loose-leaf notebook. Your résumé is the frontispiece, followed by proof. Vary the proof. A writer's might have: press releases, pamphlets, feature articles, interspersed with testimonial letters. An artist's: rough as well as finished work, only a few of each, selected to show different techniques. *Label* everything; you may be asked to leave it for a day, and you won't be there to say you won a prize for this sketch or did the research, not the copy, for that booklet.

PAVE THE WAY. Arrange for interviews with companies you want to work for. Plan carefully; don't drop in. That is good sense and good timing—people don't try to sell you something in the middle of the night. If you drop in, you are interrupting; you may be seen but perhaps with only half an eye.

Telephone or, if you are making appointments from campus, write a brief letter including your résumé. Get the *name* of the person to write to. Say why you are writing (to ask for an appointment to discuss a job), give some of your background (I expect to get my A.B. in English, can type 55 words a minute, and want to learn public relations), your plans (I shall be available in June), when you would like the interview (I shall be free the week of March 30), what action you expect of him (I am enclosing a postcard with alternate dates for your convenience in answering; or if there is no time for him to answer—I shall telephone your secretary for an appointment). This letter should be typed, dated, on business stationery, and signed, your name typed under the signature if it is illegible. Include your address.

STAGE YOUR APPOINTMENTS. The interview is the most important single thing you do, although you can jeopardize the job anywhere along the line by an untidy letter or by being late for appointments.

Part of the planning also includes finding out something about the company, which you should have done when you compiled your list of prospects. You can find out more if, as you sit in the waiting room, you read the materials there that tell about the firm, rather than the latest picture magazine. Keep this knowledge of the company in your head ready for use at the appropriate time. Don't hold a copy of the house organ blatantly under your arm.

As you are ushered into the employer's office, have an opening remark ready, such as "I appreciate your seeing me at this busy time." That breaks the ice for both of you. Be ready for him to toss the conversation to you, or to say, "Tell me about yourself," which won't be disconcerting if you have thought about it ahead of time. Your letter which led to the interview would be a good starting point; all he wants is to hear how you would give a verbal run-down of your experience. If you haven't sent him a résumé, have a copy with you in case you are asked for it, but do not produce it spontaneously—he may read it rather than listen to you. He will ask questions and answer yours. Find out all you can, but leave discussion of salary, hours, vacations, benefits until the end.

Watch for the cue that tells you the interview is over—his shoving your letter across the desk, thanking you for coming in, pushing back his chair. Then leave quickly—don't take forever buttoning your coat. And know which of you is to make the next move. Follow up the interview with a brief thank-you letter unless it was an assembly-line type of interview. You might say what you got out of it. This letter will make you stand out from other job hunters.

So much for the method of approach if you know what you want.

IF YOU DON'T KNOW WHAT YOU WANT. To reach your goal you must keep your eye on it; this requires knowing what it is. In school we were taught that the way to draw a straight line freehand is to look at the end point, not at the line being drawn. So it is with your job hunt. If you haven't your eye on something, you won't reach it directly.

You need to do some research to find out what the job market holds. Go to the public library. Read books on jobs; trade journals for happenings in the specific field, impressions of a particular firm gathered from its advertising, ideas of where openings might occur; annual reports which outline a company's accomplishments and plans; brochures which describe a business, its personnel policies, its plant; directories: *Thomas' Register of American Manufacturers* gives names of executives, while the telephone book and classified directory are invaluable for lists; and newspapers. (One applicant for a fund-raising job who watched the papers carefully read of an organization planning a new building. She wrote, enclosed her résumé, and offered her services in helping to raise the money for the building. She was hired.) Also get in touch with the trade associations in the fields you are considering.

Your reading of books and journals teaches you vocabulary and names. If you want publishing you should know the meaning of trade books and production; you will be more convincing if you are aware of the names of well-known publishing houses.

For advance information about a city unknown to you, ask the Chamber of Commerce of that state to send you data on its industries and wage scales. If you want to find out what parts of the country have certain kinds of jobs, the *Occupational Outlook Handbook* is a good reference, and includes job descriptions and employment trends.

Cautions: Don't think classified ads tell the whole story. They show the needs but may be misleading. Along with high salaries might go inconvenient locations or difficult working conditions. And keep in mind the difference between a job and a job that is open. You will learn about actual jobs, but what you want may not be available at your location and salary when you are ready.

A search of the market via your job interviews should help to clarify your job wishes. It should prevent you from being like the senior who went to see about an opinion research job and was asked what aspect interested her. She had to admit she didn't know what the aspects were; she was applying only because her psychology professor had advised her to.

Keep a record of your job hunt on cards; note the people

you see, dates, steps taken, outcome. This file will keep your lines untangled, and may be useful in later years.

DRESS CORRECTLY.   Wear something simple, neat, in season, unfrilly, and not noisy bracelets. Make sure your hair is in place. A hat isn't necessary, but wear it if you have one. Don't overdo the make-up, but don't neglect it either. Like the well-typed term paper, appearance can do wonders for you. Better not to smoke.

PROVE YOURSELF.   Whatever your field, begin the job before you are hired. A deft job hunter will apply in her search the methods and skills she hopes to apply to her job. An artist's résumé will be laid out to lead the eye down the page— her portfolio a work of art itself. The letters of a prospective proofreader will be faultless; a would-be secretary will be grammatical; a file clerk's application will have the right things in the right place.

LOOK AHEAD.   Now consider some things that are not directly connected with the job itself. First your goal. Why do you want the job? It is wise not to have too many reasons. If you are going to New York because of its concerts and museums, admit that once you get there, you have achieved that goal; don't stand in your own way and also try to get the perfect job *and* high salary. If your aim is to be a teacher, live at home and take a low-paying apprenticeship that will be good training and experience, instead of moving away and taking a less suitable job to support yourself.

Keep in mind your long-range goal too. New graduates are often asked what they hope to be doing five years from now. The answer used to be "editor for a publisher of college textbooks" or "research chemist in oil by-products." Today the answer is "married." The job is now looked upon as more or less temporary. But even if you do leave in a few years, you may be back.

Career now often means a job, then marriage, then a job again. So the question becomes, "What do you hope to be doing after your youngest child is in school and you want to get out of the house?" Today women are returning to work after raising families, and what is significant to you is that returners are beginners all over again, inexperienced or with rusty skills. They must start at the bottom and they, naturally, don't like the prospect. So let the first thing you do start you toward what you want to come back to—a job that gives you training that can be brought up to date later, or an advanced degree that enables you to step back in.

Statistics tell us that you will probably work for twenty-one years of your life if you marry and have a family, for forty years if you stay single. These figures show the reason for advance planning. When you do marry, keep your hand in. Continue your association memberships, read the journals, attend meetings, take courses. When you undertake volunteer work, make it meaningful: look for assignments you can do well and contribute to—ideally something that can be applied to a paid job someday in the future. Be conscientious about it. Your professional attitude can raise the status of volunteers to the level it deserves, and dispel some of the skepticism.

YOU ARE MOVING TO A STRANGE CITY? Then go prepared for the job you want. Beware of big cities that have many jobs; they attract other people too and the jobs may be taken. Apartments may be scarce or expensive; or landlords refuse you because you might not stay.

Precious time and money are lost by those who arrive unequipped and then concentrate on looking instead of preparing. Don't put your placement counselors in the false position of trying to help you find *any* job. And don't assume that generalizations about jobs apply to every part of the country. Consult local employment sources to learn what the picture is there. Being qualified means being able to fit current job openings; it does not mean having a wealth of experience.

Then consider the budget. Think over your expenses. List

obvious things like rent, food, clothing. Lunches, bus fares, and cleaners' bills add up quickly; and when you do get an apartment, you must pay for supplies, laundry, electricity, telephone. Then make yourself think of the unexpected. Suppose you go to the theatre, it rains, and you have to take a taxi you hadn't planned on? Or you break a tooth and get a large dental bill? You needn't put down exact amounts; just be conscious of what the items might include. With a budget made out, you will be better able to plan expenses and interpret salary offers.

In gauging salaries, allow for social security, federal income tax, perhaps state income tax, and other withholdings that make your take-home pay smaller than your earnings. See what you actually receive after the minimum of withholdings:

WHAT YOU ACTUALLY GET IN YOUR PAY CHECK
(if you are single, with one exemption)

Weekly Salary Earned	$70.00	
Less Federal Income Tax		$10.50
Less Social Security		2.54
Weekly Amount Taken Home	$56.96	
Weekly Salary Earned	$80.00	
Less Federal Income Tax		$12.30
Less Social Security		2.90
Weekly Amount Taken Home	$64.80	
Weekly Salary Earned	$100.00	
Less Federal Income Tax		$16.10
Less Social Security		3.63 *
Weekly Amount Taken Home	$ 80.27	

This table includes the minimum withholdings.
There may be others.

* Deducted only from the first $4,800 of your salary.

THE PRICE TAG IS ON THE JOB, NOT ON YOU. Job hunters sometimes use the wrong measuring stick in judging starting salaries. Many factors go into determining what you will be offered:

—the economic situation: recessions decrease some salaries;
—the employer's budget and personnel policies: he may have a standard salary for new employees;
—the section of the country: there may be a labor surplus.

So if your roommate is making more than you are offered, the dollar value may not be a fair comparison. Besides, take into consideration fringe benefits which add a lot that doesn't show. The free tuition courses a university allows its employees actually represent tax-free income. And remember, salaries do go up.

Don't pay too much for salary. An interesting and appropriate job at lower pay may be worth it.

CARRYING RESPONSIBILITY MEANS CARRYING IT. If you are aiming high, start early by finding out what is ahead. Being an executive is more than a title on the door. The head of a company or department is a servant, not a master. Requests of others must be listened to. In our democratic society you consult everyone concerned, study alternatives, and then follow the majority opinion. You don't just delegate. If the receptionist isn't there to open the office, deliver an envelope, or answer the telephone, you may have to.

Being an executive means interruptions; sometimes you will think you do more of other people's work than of your own. When you are in the midst of adding a column of numbers or groping for a word, someone may come in with a question or the telephone will ring. You must accept these interruptions.

An executive will get credit but also blame. You'll swallow your pride and write apologies for things you had nothing to do with. Long days, evening meetings, weekend conventions are all part of executive work. When you close your desk it is only a gesture; your mind, if not your brief case, may remain full of tomorrow's problems.

WHAT'S AGAINST YOU.   An important reason women are not hired as fast or promoted as far as they would like is that they won't stay. Of course they won't. A woman's first job is her family. And gradually employers are learning where women can be useful in spite of their temporary working capacity. But just the same, women themselves must recognize their liabilities.

Sometimes it seems as though you can't win. Some employers hesitate to hire women who are single because they will leave to get married; others won't hire married women because they will leave to have children. Recently a girl was in tears after weeks of job hunting: nobody would hire her because she was engaged.

Women can help by being professional when accepting or giving up a job. Some take on permanent jobs knowing they will leave in a few months. Teachers resign, breaking their contracts at a moment's notice when their husbands are transferred. Yet the husbands who insist on this resignation would not condone it in their own employees. Don't take the easy out and say that in our society it is the custom for wives to follow their husbands.

Conventional objections to hiring a woman evaporate if your attitude is right. That means you are willing to do whatever is asked—take a preparatory course before you are hired, accept a lesser job, or work difficult hours at first. The person who raises objections, wants all her demands met, is afraid a job is beneath her, will lose out because she is unwilling, not because she is unqualified. One 81-year-old applicant found a job after only a week of looking because she followed every suggestion given to her; age never stood in her way.

The right attitude includes being on time (making up for lateness by staying after five o'clock isn't the same thing; your employer wants you there during business hours for questions or sudden assignments) and good attendance: don't overdo absences for minor aches—you won't get concessions when the real thing comes along.

It has been said that good manners on the road automatically mean safe drivers. Good manners applied to all aspects of your search go a long way to make you professional, and your job hunt successful.

III

CLERICAL AND SECRETARIAL

Clerical jobs range from those of the receptionist to those of the secretary. In 1960, 2.4 million persons were employed in these occupations, and 95 per cent were women.

The minimum requirement is high school. Education, ability, and experience bring advancement. The highest salaries are in large cities on the West Coast and in the North Central area; the lowest are in the South. The field that pays the highest is manufacturing.

RECEPTIONIST

A *receptionist* is a greeter and therefore has a coveted job. She may sit at a desk just inside the door of an office, or at the elevator-entrance of a business that has a whole floor, or at the main entrance of a building. She asks visitors' names and business, notifies the person they have come to see (by interoffice telephone), asks them to wait or to go in, hangs up their coats, sometimes escorts them in. In large offices she may keep a daily record of appointments, when they came, whom they saw. In some cases she is also the switchboard operator; in others she types envelopes, folds and stuffs letters, if her regular duties don't keep her occupied. In small offices she may be a secretary with receptionist duties.

She must be attractive, but more. Dignified, affable, tactful in the right amounts. She must know which visitors to greet cordially, which to turn away firmly, which to mollify. Often mature women are sought for these jobs on executive floors.

She must enjoy variety and the unexpected, take stretches of inactivity alternating with onslaughts of many visitors and equally many demands. She will meet solicitors, salesmen, job hunters. She may order sandwiches, pin up falling hems, baby-sit while a mother sees her lawyer, soothe a worried patient.

Here is a job for those who want clearly defined hours, a pleasant atmosphere, few technical requirements, and much contact with people.

If the job is combined with secretarial work, it can lead anywhere in commercial, professional, and non-profit organizations and in factories. If the duties are purely receptionist, it is a job in itself. But remember that when a receptionist is outside the hub of the office activity, she won't observe and learn what goes on in the business.

FILE CLERK

Filing means putting away letters, reports, clippings, plans, blueprints, charts, and other papers according to a system that enables you to find them again. It is not just a manual or rote operation. A creative *file clerk* reads and knows what she is putting away, when to file alphabetically, chronologically, geographically, by subject, by the name of a person, when to make a cross reference (a note in the other logical places indicating what category a paper is filed under). Some filing is done by ear as well as eye (an unintelligible name reported by a foreign-speaking witness is classified according to all possible spellings of that sound).

File supervisors who oversee the work of the clerks must know the rules of filing, be able to train the employees, check their work.

TYPIST

A *typist* produces one or more copies of letters, reports, manuscripts, speeches, advertising material, statistical tables or budgets on a machine. She may work from neatly typed material or from much-corrected, written-over, and x-ed out pages, or from a dictating machine where she listens to a record or tape on a light earpiece. She must handle paper and carbons, make unsmudged corrections, know her machine, keep it clean, be able to change its ribbon, understand its simple failings.

The work is mechanical, but the job is not. Typing requires concentration (good typists could not pass a reading test on what they have typed); the ability to gauge space: where to start on a page, whether to single or double space; an eye for design. An inventive person finds several variations for the same copy, if she is allowed leeway. She must be neat and orderly, good at spelling, grammar, punctuation.

Forty-five words a minute is generally the minimum requirement for beginners; jobs for the experienced ask for more. Test yourself before you apply, so that you don't jeopardize a job by risking failure on the employer's test. Do better than the minimum on your own trusty portable; the machine you are tested on may seem like an unmanageable monster.

You can specialize in varityping, a machine that makes margins come out evenly, or in statistical typing, all figure work.

It is never too soon to learn to type; start typing in your schooldays if you can. Learn the touch system, in which you know the keys by position, without having to look at them. The hunt-and-peck method may satisfy your early needs, but for business you must be professional; manage to learn the right method at the start and not have to unlearn another.

Typewriters are manual and electric. These terms refer

to the way they are powered; your job is the same on both. Electric machines go faster and need only a light touch.

There are typewriters made for left-handed and right-handed people, and special ones for those who can use only one hand. The shift keys, back spacer, carriage return are placed at the more convenient side.

SECRETARY

A *secretary* is everything that other office assistants are and more besides. Part of that more includes taking dictation, usually by stenography. Shorthand systems are found useful every day by all of us: isn't 245 Broadway faster to write than Two Hundred Forty-five Broadway? A secretary's shorthand is a system of abbreviated symbols (unless she uses a dictating machine). When she just takes dictation and transcribes her notes, she is a *stenographer*. Court stenographers make verbatim reports of conferences or court proceedings by shorthand or on a stenotype machine (similar to a small typewriter on a portable stand).

A secretary also operates other office machines: mimeograph, addressograph, postage meter, folding, copying. She opens mail, acknowledges it from instructions or on her own, attends to inquiries, sends for materials, perhaps does simple bookkeeping, makes bank deposits, keeps track of office supplies. Actual duties vary with the business, but they are much broader than the purely stenographic. She works with clerks, executives, salesmen, printers, reservation agents, reporters, caterers. She is on the inside track, deals with private information, is both a representative and a protector.

Secretarial skills can give you:

—training for a new career—when you are starting out or returning to work;

—a beginning in a new town—if your husband is transferred you can more easily find a job;

—insurance—a Broadway actress once said that shorthand and typing were the best preparation for the stage—those in the performing arts, or in any field, need not be unemployed between engagements;

—cash in the bank—you can pick up secretarial jobs as a temporary sideline if you want to expand your income;

—retirement benefits—a way to save for later years.

There is a wide choice of jobs for those who can type, a wider one for those with shorthand; and salaries rise with each additional skill. High salaries go to court stenographers, to those who specialize (legal, medical, bilingual), and to executive and administrative secretaries.

Secretarial skills are an open sesame. For those who want a career in any field that has to do with words (publishing, public relations, radio, television, advertising, journalism), they are a must, tools of the trade. Reporters bang out their copy, authors think on the typewriter, advertising agencies train you into copy by having you type others'. One girl said she pitied the boys who had to get their training in the mail room while she was learning by doing.

Will you get stuck? Not if you play it right. Choose a suitable company (heavy industry is less apt to promote women out of a clerical category); choose your man (if he has a reputation for hoarding his secretary, don't let him get hold of you); choose the field you want to advance in—since you are going ahead in any case, be on the right track.

Secretarial work may not be for *you*. Slow readers and poor spellers should consider another opening wedge. And if your interests are in merchandising, banking, insurance, investments, or market research, their training courses or other beginning jobs may be the promotion spots. You aren't expected to make the decision yourself; employment counselors can advise you.

But even if you are using secretarial skills as a stepping stone, be conscientious about the job while you have it, and don't start looking over the fence immediately. Camilla L became a secretary in a public relations office while hoping for a quick promotion. Impatience made her careless. In the first week she handed her boss two letters where the carbon had been put in backwards. When he pointed it out she thought it amusing; he fired her for her attitude. Do your best at the job you are hired for; don't be an ostrich and hide your skills hoping to avoid using them.

While on the job, keep your eyes open for ways to get ahead. Offer to read a manuscript or to look up information or draft a letter—suggestions that cut red tape, save time or money can bring promotions.

Some take shorthand and typing for their own use, not for their employers'. One, the assistant to a theatrical manager, studied shorthand at night so that she could get his rapid instructions. Now she can call rehearsals quickly, order the right costumes, check attendance. One publishing vice president, afraid to lose her shorthand and thereby be shorthanded at meetings, translates subway advertisements to keep in trim. The head of a large university hospital is the envy of his wife, also an executive, because he composes his lectures on the typewriter while she trudges through hers in longhand.

A secretary may have any of a number of titles: secretary, girl or gal Friday, office assistant, typist. She might also be a personnel assistant, editorial trainee, or writer. Many secretaries complain that they don't use their shorthand after having been advised to learn it; they should remember, it did enable them to get the job.

A secretary may work in a small office shared with her boss, a large room with dozens of others, or in a separate one by herself. She may have employers who shout at her, demand more than she can do, give her a letter at five of five. Because she is so much in demand, her starting salary is better than that of most jobs, and can go high.

The job is also an end in itself, an important position. An executive or administrative secretary or assistant carries responsibility, prestige. She gives more orders than she takes, is sometimes her boss's boss—sets up his schedule, tells him when he may go to lunch, reminds him of commitments. She may be office manager, delegate work, make decisions.

Automation may change the duties but will probably not affect the demand. A man likes you because you smile when taking dictation (machines are chilly), know which telephone messages to bury at the bottom of the pile, what callers he is out to.

Examples of successes are myriad. All around you are editors, heads of copy departments, research directors, public relations executives, business owners who began as secretaries. One, through office skills, has been executive secretary to an ambassador and to a president's wife.

OFFICE SERVICES

A new type of business has come to the fore in recent years. This is the temporary office service which provides office workers for peak periods that cannot be handled by permanent staffs. Clerks, typists, secretaries can get jobs by the day, week, or month in every kind of business. These services are in large cities all over the country.

When you sign up with one, you are tested and then classified according to your ability which determines your rate of pay. The service acts as your employer, and pays your wages (less than if you had found the job yourself), though you actually work for another office.

Using these sources is a good way to get a stopgap job or to learn what different fields are like.

For Further Information about Jobs or Training

The National Secretaries Association (International), 1103 Grand Avenue, Suite 410, Kansas City 6, Missouri

United Business Education Association (Department of the National Education Association), 1201–16th Street, Washington 6, D.C.

IV

NON-PROFESSIONAL JOBS WITHIN THE PROFESSIONS

To make a sound decision about your vocation, you should have all the facts. You may want to go into a profession, and yet have given up the idea because you have neither the graduate degree nor the cash to get it. And so you turn to business to tide yourself over. But it would get you on your way sooner and add up to more in the end if you started toward your profession at once. You can do this in a number of beginning spots provided you have the preliminary requirements.

It might be wise to get a look at the field before launching on it, since you may find it is not for you after all. Any job that puts you in the milieu can give you a view of the field; even a negative result can help both you and the profession.

Some jobs can be an end in themselves for the professionally minded who are giving no thought to graduate degrees. And such people are in good company. John Glenn was a test pilot, at the technician level, not an engineer; he did not graduate from college; and he was 40 when he maneuvered *Friendship VII* through space!

This chapter will take a quick look at some of the beginning jobs in the professions, with notes about further graduate school education necessary to obtain professional standing.

Just about all of these jobs require a college degree. Always check further with local and current requirements.

Archaeology. Assistants make surveys and contour maps, label items, and dig—a real shovel-and-trowel job, detailed, careful, aching.

A.B. in Archaeology. Ph.D. for advancement.

Architecture. Apprentices, under experienced draftsmen, letter plans, make working drawings of details for layouts; checkers examine drawings for errors. Landscape architecture, a better field for women, involves making sketches, estimating costs, and preparing drawings for developments.

A.A. from a junior college for junior draftsmen. A.B. and graduate degrees needed for the profession.

Art. Lecturer, information clerk, or guide in the information department of museums; secretary in their editorial or membership department and for curators, and in the history of art departments in colleges.

Biology. Laboratory assistant—in hospitals, medical research organizations, and food and drug industries—does laboratory tests, takes notes for doctors. Museum aide in natural history museums helps arrange displays, conducts tours, answers questions, explains exhibits.

Bachelor's degree in biology or an allied science needed for starting jobs; further degrees needed for research.

Chemistry. Laboratory assistant washes bottles, makes tests and measurements, analyzes chemical contents of materials, uses litmus paper and flame-color tests for identification, keeps notes on progress of experiments. In industry, there are jobs for a library assistant as well: opening mail, deciding what to do with it—file it, send it to an executive doing a paper, or toss it.

Bachelor's degree in Chemistry. Advanced degrees needed for research.

City Planning. Planners gather and summarize data on population trends or use of land; study needs of tenants evicted for an urban renewal project; draft plans for future development, present them to the community, prepare exhibits. Start with city and regional planning associations or government agencies.

A.B. in Planning, with courses in architecture and public administration preferred. Economics and Government majors are sometimes accepted. The best future requires an M.A.

Dance. Teacher in recreational centers, settlement houses, ballroom dancing schools. For ways to get into the field, try summer stock, night clubs, local operas, industrial productions, even setting up your own classes for children. Probably no performers are permanently employed.

A.B. advisable for teaching and performing, plus study at professional schools or music academies; or private lessons at an early age and then advanced classes.

Dental Hygienist. The work includes making charts for final diagnosis by dentist, mixing filling compounds, preparing solutions, cleaning and polishing teeth, massaging gums, sterilizing instruments, educating parents on care of children's teeth and on diets; the hygienist may make appointments and keep records as well.

High school graduate, sometimes three years of college, to qualify for two-year training course leading to license.

Dental Technician makes casts, artificial teeth, crowns, bridges; works from molds; polishes and finishes dentures. Deals with prescriptions, not patients.

No educational requirement, but four years of training on the job.

Geology. Openings occur with the government in work on map revisions, or in laboratories. Not a good spot for women because of heavy field work.

Bachelor's degree in Geology; graduate degrees needed for research.

Home Economics. There are opportunities to buy, or do comparison shopping for stores, or test materials for shrinking, fading, raveling; demonstrate kitchen equipment; test recipes sent to food manufacturer by the public; arrange dishes for pictures on packages, take photographs, write copy.

Bachelor's degree in Home Economics.

Law.   Those interested in the legal field and not going into it professionally can get close to it just the same. Law firms hire English majors for proofreading. Any major, with intelligence and insight, can be a legal file clerk, virtually a library job: collect documents, briefs, exhibits, for a coming trial, see that all are there, label them, look up information, put materials away.

Some lawyers lean on their secretary for a good deal of help; they ask her instead of a newly hired law school graduate to draft a deed or will because she has done it for years and needs no instruction.

Library Work.   Beginners are clerks, typists, messengers. Get books from the shelves, put them away, look up titles, authors, subjects, prepare books for the binder, answer questions, record books borrowed and returned, type catalogue cards, send notices of overdue books, read stories to children, set up exhibits.

Jobs are in public libraries (not musty any more, those are on the way out), and special libraries, which are libraries of individual subjects—insurance, banking, advertising, education, art.

A.B. in any major to start, a degree in Library Science (L.S.) for the profession; advanced degrees in subject matter for some special librarians.

Medical Technician   makes chemical, microscopic, blood, bacteriological, and skin tests, determines blood type, examines tissue samples. Findings form the basis of doctors' and surgeons' diagnoses.

A.B. and additional year of hospital training leading to B.S.

Medicine—Other Jobs.   Receptionist and secretary in doctors' offices or in service organizations which set up files, make out bills, do bookkeeping and accounting for physicians. Editorial assistant, with typing, in advertising agencies handling medical accounts or on medical publications. Hospital interviewer to collect information from patients for research studies.

A.B. preferred.

Music.   Give private lessons at home or in studios; sing or play the organ in church or the piano in department stores or at skating rinks; lead community singing. Secretarial jobs with record companies can lead to the designing of jackets or the writing of their blurbs; secretarial work for concert artists' management bureaus can lead to public relations, talent selling, arranging tours.

A.B. in Music Education or in Music, or private study with an accomplished artist or in a conservatory of music. Advanced study needed for performer, arranger, composer, librettist, music librarian.

Nurse's Aide carries out simple nursing tasks: makes beds, bathes patients, delivers messages, counts linen, escorts patients around hospital.

No starting requirement; training given on the job.

Occupational Therapist.   The uses of educational and recreational activities for the sick, injured, disabled. Formerly, such therapy included only handcrafts and arts meant to combat boredom during illness or convalescence; today it stresses business and industrial skills as well. Therapist must know the patient's capacity and ability: sculpture may involve muscles he cannot use, while painting does not.

A beginner can teach her own subject—ceramics, music, photography. Jobs are in hospitals, mental institutions, sanitariums, vocational rehabilitation centers, schools for the handicapped.

Bachelor's degree and one year of graduate work in occupational therapy, then a year's interneship.

Physical Therapist applies heat, light, water, electricity, massage, and exercise to treat injuries and diseases of muscles and bones. Also teaches the use of braces and crutches.

Bachelor's degree in a science or in Physical Education, plus a year and a half of graduate work leading to a certificate.

Physics. Beginner assists in industrial research laboratories (does a wire with a spherical cross section conduct electricity faster than one with a triangular one?), or with space agencies and other government offices; writes instruction manuals for new equipment.

Bachelor's degree in Physics. Graduate degrees needed for research.

Practical Nurse gives treatments and medicine, takes temperature, pulse, blood pressure, and makes routine laboratory tests in hospitals, health agencies, and at homes for chronic or convalescent patients or the aged.

Two years of high school. Training lasts nine to eighteen months.

Psychology. Psychometrists administer, score, interpret tests, and write reports on them for department stores, women's specialty shops, mail-order houses, public utility companies, the government, and other areas. Business personnel assistants, if they have had statistics, do research on personnel problems—studies of turnover, working conditions, output; they interview employees, analyze results, draw graphs. Assistants in organizations that make and sell standardized tests draft trial questions, test them, determine reliability of new tests. Jobs also include receptionists in vocational counseling offices.

Requirements for psychologists have been getting continually stiffer because of the abuse of the title.

Minimum requirement is an M.A. in Psychology. To call yourself a psychologist you must have a Ph.D. and pass a certifying examination.

Recreation. Assistant supervisors referee games, lead adult dances, introduce newcomers, entertain children, teach music and crafts at camps, playgrounds, community recreation centers, beaches, churches, hotels, hospitals. Often evening and weekend work is involved.

A.B. in Sociology or Psychology. Graduate degrees needed for advancement.

Religion. Work is available for pastors' assistants, secretaries in churches or in religious organizations, teachers of religious education, editorial assistants for religious publications.

A.B. in Philosophy or Religion for most openings.

Social Work. Investigators for state welfare departments interview familes applying for relief, make recommendations. Office assistants in social service offices of hospitals, church organizations, or public and private welfare offices (like adoption services, family and health centers, orphanages) do secretarial work.

Group work is often as near as you can get to social work without a graduate degree. District directors act as liaison between community, parents, and teachers in programs of national women's and children's organizations. Case aides in mental institutions and probation offices work with families and ease the transition back to daily life.

A.B. in a social science. Master's Degree in Social Service Work needed for the profession. County welfare offices have programs in which you study while you work, but if you stop in the middle of the program, you sometimes have to refund that part of the salary which represented tuition. Some states let you do casework without a graduate degree, but this experience is no substitute for the degree in other states.

Teaching. Apprentice or student teachers can find openings in independent schools; substitute teachers with temporary emergency licenses are employed by public schools. Reading counselors, hired by specialized reading organizations, teach improvement of reading techniques to students and executives.

Bachelor's degree generally needed. Public school requirements vary from state to state, but a certificate is necessary, which requires one year after college.

Theatre. Summer theatre, amateur parts, walk-on bits on television are starting footholds, though many aspirants for the stage support themselves through office jobs. Secretarial openings with playwrights, producers, theatre associations, advertising agencies' TV departments, and local radio stations may lead to acting. An unusual application of theatrical interest: puppeteering. Give shows for TV, window advertising, night clubs.

V

ADVERTISING

A girl is typing a report for the research department of an advertising agency. During the past week, she interviewed applicants for the job of polling magazine readers about a specific ad; tabulated results from questionnaires; went to the library for information on production and sales. She is a *secretary*, interested in statistics, and hopes to advance in this department.

Advertising informs potential customers of the advantages of goods or services. The advertising agency studies the product, the potential market, methods of sales and distribution, formulates a plan of action, and then executes the plan. The work entails a great deal more than the deft copy and dynamic picture we see as consumers. Sometimes agencies provide free advertising help to non-profit organizations and civic efforts (campaigns for a cleaner city, safe driving, conservation of water). Sometimes they make suggestions to help business: Bolts, Inc., a manufacturer of yard goods, was advised to change its name to Cloth, Inc. to avoid confusion.

A PREFERENCE FOR NUMBERS. The research secretary got her job because her college marks in sociology were good, she had some interviewing experience as an undergraduate, and she agreed to study statistics. Others in her department started as *interviewers* and *tabulators,* a more usual beginning.

The agency has taken on a new account, a detergent. Before a plan is drafted, the agency finds out if: people like the product, find it useful, have mistaken impressions about it which advertising copy or a change in label-color could dispel. The report the secretary is typing gives the answers.

On other studies it was not consumers who were questioned, but salesmen, retailers, and wholesalers who count sales. From them the research department learned the kinds of people who buy the detergent and where they live (rural low-income families like it because it is cheaper than others on the market). From the laboratory came information about uses of this detergent (especially good for ink stains), advantages over similar products (a pleasant odor).

Down the hall, also statistics-minded, is a *secretary in the media department.* Her desk is strewn with the standard order blanks which agencies use to place ads with newspapers, magazines, buses, radio, television (the media). She is learning her way through the reports of the Standard Rate and Data Service which gives charges and mechanical requirements of media; the Audit Bureau of Circulations (ABC) on the number of cars that pass certain points; reports of areas covered by broadcasting networks and passengers carried by transit companies. She measures inches and seconds, dollars and cents. The head of her department must find the most efficient medium to enable the ad to reach the largest number of potential buyers (not a subway poster for a diamond necklace), in the best market (cities for high-heeled shoes).

Also for the numerically inclined are jobs in the checking, billing, and paying departments. Before the agency pays for an ad, it must be sure it really did appear. As proof, the magazine or newspaper produces a tear sheet or the whole publication; stations send an affidavit or certificate of performance. These are compared with the order (size, date, frequency), then the bill is cleared or an adjustment requested.

ROOM FOR WRITERS.   The copywriting department turns out the printed material (copy), slogans, booklets, posters, direct mail. Copy must be clear, easily understood, appealing. The type of approach varies with the medium. Magazine buyers have time to read testimonial ads, but motorists can take in only brief captions on billboard pictures.

What does the *copywriter* do to make the product sell? She has facts to help her sing different praises. A large car carries more passengers, is more comfortable; a smaller car can be parked in less space, is more economical.

The *secretary in the copy department* keeps files, relays finished copy to the art department, may do research, sees how differently magazine copy and television commercials are written. She has what it takes to progress here: skill in the use of words and an understanding of people. She knows it is not enough just to be able to express herself; she must know how her audience behaves. She has taken courses in writing and psychology. She observes the way art work and copy must complement each other. Once a television commercial used dancing figures that were so eye-catching that the name of the sponsoring product was unnoticed!

GOAL: COPYWRITER.   A copywriter should produce strong proof of her interest and ability along this line, not only because the job is exacting, but because it is popular. It helps if you majored or minored in English, a sign of interest, not ability. Make up a portfolio of your writing samples from the school yearbook or college paper; cut out ads you think are effective and write a paragraph explaining why. Draft some ads yourself, but be prepared for some agencies to dislike this idea and feel your errors distract them.

Annette Y went to a junior college and into advertising immediately as a trainee with a large New York agency. She had an unusual flair for writing and learned the technique fast. She also had a stick-to-itiveness that took her far. Soon she was writing copy for such varied accounts as baby powder, underwear, and facial tissues. She then moved on to another agency where she covered coffee and cereal ads besides radio commercials for soaps. She grew to be a senior copywriter and then associate copy director, with a salary in five figures. Twenty years after college she hung out her own shingle as a copy consultant.

The publicity department is another for writers. It writes news about a redesigned trademark, an account just received, an executive promotion, a policy change; it makes the agency known.

A PLACE FOR ARTISTS.   In another office, a girl has a pencil behind her ear, fingers sticky from glue, a desk covered with pieces of paper, bottles of rubber cement, compass, scissors, ruler, eraser, photographs, and heavily penciled sheets; passers-by tease her about cutting out paper dolls. She is a *secretary in the art department,* learning its ways. She envies the *paste-up girl* who was hired before her without office skills, but she knows such openings are rare.

The secretary went to a liberal arts college, majored in painting, does oils. She is seeing how the *art director* coordinates the picture, slogan, trade name, message. Answer: trial and error. Rough sketches show the arrangement of an illustration with the text. Horizontal lines indicate where the words go, quick roughs outline a picture (probably to be supplied by an outside artist or studio, not a member of the staff). She tries variations, may find the type size cramps the picture, the number of type faces give a restless effect, or margins are too narrow. Sometimes she wants to change only one element (move the product name from upper left to center); she does not redo the whole page, but merely glues the revised parts over the original. Color changes are tested by overlaying tinted transparent sheets. When the final layout is done she may duplicate it by a photographic process and send it to different departments for suggestions or approval. She knows that the glued edges will not be picked up by the camera; that her blue penciled instructions for the printer will not show in the photograph.

The secretary's work includes designs for booklets, packages, folders, displays, mechanicals (layouts to show a client), story boards (series of sketches planning the steps of a TV commercial).

She learns how to mesh layouts, scale work, and fit photographs, along with cleaning pastepots, sharpening pencils, writing letters. She is in touch with commercial artists, photographers, retouchers, type experts, engravers, production men. Since she wants to get ahead, she is taking art courses, attending exhibits, keeping up with the latest trends in design. She will learn to letter with pencil or brush, condense or expand different type faces, hand-letter testimonials, buy art work, judge samples submitted by free-lance illustrators, get permission to reproduce pictures, set up a file of photographs and paintings. She will study the techniques of painting so as to be able to give practicable directions.

Down the hall from her, manned by people with typography and printing backgrounds, is the production department, which will get her finished product after it has been approved, and put it into print. The actual reproducing is done elsewhere, but here the secretary orders paper and plates. The *head of the production department* knows printing, engraving, lithography, typography, electrotyping, phototyping.

One of the jobs of this department is to see that things are done on time. Therefore when the secretary applied for her job, she said she could handle a flood of details under pressure, and proved it by describing how she once managed an overnight camping trip for six nine-year-old boys, including food, transportation, supervision, and coped with the sudden return caused by rain.

EXPEDITING.   With so many pieces to put together, a system is needed to insure the meeting of deadlines. Traffic control

Rough Layout for an Ad Showing Position
of Illustration and Copy

(or traffic department), sometimes the print production department, fills this need. Forms are used to see that the art work, copy or commercials, and plates are prepared on schedule, that client and lawyer approve, and that the final product reaches the medium on time. This job requires a mind for details, a sense of organization, an inner clock, and ability to needle people without their knowing it.

The coordinator and catalyst of the entire process is the *account executive,* an advertising position not frequently held by women.

The work of the account executive covers the before, during, and after of the operation. She finds prospects, drafts the presentation (verbal and graphic), lands the account, draws up the campaign, oversees it, keeps the client constantly informed. She must know all phases of selling, advertising, marketing, merchandising, and perhaps also have a knowledge of a particular field. She attends sales conventions and knows her way around the world of the client.

The beginner in this department must be gracious, accurate, communicative, systematic. She relays information from one department to another and follows up on the standing of the different accounts.

IF YOU HAVE SPECIAL INTERESTS. You can use advertising as a way of applying a particular subject. *Artists* can work in the fashion department, keep abreast of the current styles, watch forecasts, recommend and choose clothes, accessories, backdrops for still photographs or filmed commercials.

If show business excites you, the radio and television department handles the developing, producing, directing of a show or a commercial, including the writing and editing of scripts, recording, casting and paying the talent, scheduling and publicizing. Sometimes package producers supply the story, format, performers, sets, musicians, director—the agency's job being to sell a show to the client, supervise it, negotiate for air time, create the commercials. Or else the networks and stations produce the program, while the agency selects a show and recommends it to the client. Beginners should have run the straw-hat circuit or worked in school dramatics, be musical, or have a way with photography or playwriting. They start as secretaries.

Those with international interests can work for agencies with accounts or offices in foreign countries.

In a large agency there are places for *economists*—to interpret the significance of a rise or fall in earnings or output; *lawyers*—to decide such matters as whether "thermos" is still a trade name or now in the public domain; *engineers*—an advertisement for steel, comparing its strength and durability to that of another metal, must be accurate; *psychologists*—to devise and interpret behavior tests.

If you have other interests you want to use, see the Agency List of *The Standard Advertising Register* and *McKittrick Directory of Advertisers* (Agency List).

A WORD OF WARNING.   Hours can be long and irregular, especially for account executives. Sometimes tremendous pressures accompany the work: the pace can be frantic, the atmosphere electric. Accounts move often from one agency to another and people are hired and fired accordingly. Therefore, advertising is not necessarily for those who want job security.

WHERE TO FIND THE JOBS.   Advertising agencies may be large ones with the departments outlined, or small ones with the same person doing several things. Most agencies that handle national advertising are in New York, Chicago, Detroit, Los Angeles, San Francisco, St. Louis, Cleveland, Minneapolis, Pittsburgh, and Philadelphia; many of these have branches in other cities which also have local independent agencies. Starting salaries are about the same as those in other fields, but when you reach your late twenties, if you are moving up and doing well, you will be earning more than your contemporaries elsewhere.

Women who are interested in advertising find many more openings outside the agency field. A job with an advertising department of a store is good training, and it is easier to get in here as a paste-up girl without secretarial skills than it is in an agency. Selling experience is a good way in because you learn how people respond: will the display of sunglasses at the glove counter sell more glasses or just be a nuisance to customers trying on gloves?

Very good opportunities occur in mail-order houses which hire more beginners as copywriters than does the whole agency business. Here the trick is to write copy that will interest, tell the whole story, and make the final sale.

You may also find jobs with manufacturers, distributors, and advertising media concerned with selling space rather than buying. A unique aspect of magazine advertising is direct mail: the skill is to give the current reader, who already knows the product, a reason to resubscribe. Finally, there are jobs with advertising services: printers, engravers, and supply houses.

You can bypass advertising at first and get experience in a profession. Claire N started out to be a doctor, but gave up her training when she got married. Now she writes copy for medical accounts, describing new medicines and instruments, bringing a knowledge that her colleagues would need hours to absorb.

WHAT SORT OF PEOPLE ARE SUCCESSFUL IN ADVERTISING? Women are wanted in this field because so much advertising is directed at them as the consumers. Although women have been active in all departments of agencies, the logical accounts for them are textiles, cosmetics, home furnishings, clothes, food. Some have become heads of their own agencies and advertising managers of corporations.

This field could be for you if you are ambitious, serious, sophisticated about advertising—and do not think the reception room hung with colorful and witty ads epitomizes the work. You should be open to new ideas and ways of doing things, adaptable to other people's suggestions, an individualist who works well with others. You should have many interests, hobbies, an insatiable curiosity, a real desire to solve problems. You should have a dozen ideas per square inch, ideas for the long pull, not just for one shot. Can you build three ads around your idea for naming a new overnight train Sleeper Deeper?

Susan L was assigned the job of writing jingles for musical commercials; she had no music background and found it difficult to follow directions about rhythm, pitch, beat; so she took piano lessons at night, which brought her not only a promotion, but a new interest, for she then went on to study classical music. The next thing she knew she found herself applying a sonata form to a one-minute commercial which proved to be one of the most successful on the air.

In college, if you want to start toward this field, you can take art, education, history, home economics, journalism, marketing, philosophy, psychology, science, or sociology. Your marks are more important than your major; your extracurricular work, an indication of an active person, weighs heavily in your favor. Evidence of your leadership, originality, writing ability will help you stand out. You must be willing to be anonymous; the public never knows who wrote that copy everybody is talking about.

For Further Information about Jobs or Training

The Advertising Federation of America, 655 Madison Avenue, New York 21, New York

American Association of Advertising Agencies, 420 Lexington Avenue, New York 17, New York

Association of National Advertisers, 155 East 44th Street, New York 17, New York

VI

ARMED SERVICES

There is something about a uniform. Or a band. Or the chance to contribute to the progress of your country. Whatever it is, women seek places in the armed services, learn while working, and enjoy serving.

There are opportunities to hold the same jobs in the same fields as in civilian life. If you consider the armed services as one large company with business to be transacted, publicized, accounted for, and kept supplied, its personnel hired, fed, clothed, kept healthy, moved from place to place, then you can begin to see how many different spots there can be for you. The armed services are active in peace as well as in war. Women back up the work of the men, freeing them for other tasks.

These services consist of: Wac (Woman's Army Corps), WAF (Women in the Air Force), WAVES (Women in the Navy), Women Marines, Army Nurse Corps, Navy Nurse Corps, Air Force Nurse Corps, Army Medical Specialist Corps, Air Force Medical Specialist Corps.

In order to enlist you need to be a high school graduate, at least 18 (get parent or guardian permission if you are under 21), in good health, with no dependents, and willing to sign up for two years in the Wac, three in the WAF and Marines, four in the WAVES.

Basic (boot) training is coeducational, lasts eight or nine weeks. There you learn such things as protocol, military discipline, map reading, laws of justice, how to launder uniforms and maintain good health. While each service has different regulations, in general you may not marry during training, may after that, and then must complete part of your enlistment.

After training you will be assigned to a job as near to what you want as possible. There is no guarantee you will get the job of your choice. If you don't like what you are given, you can be reclassified, but may not keep changing. You work an eight-hour day (except in emergencies), sometimes in shifts, and you will have military duties besides your regular assignments. You may be sent anywhere in the United States, or to Europe, Japan, Hawaii, Okinawa. You may not work on the combat field, or on planes or ships other than transport and hospital. You live in a dormitory, and as enlisted personnel, housekeep your own quarters.

The usual starting job in an office is *clerk, typist, stenographer.* You can do machine accounting (the application of automation to problem-solving), for which you work with key punch and verifying machines to record statistical data (the number of medical discharges issued in the previous year, or the amount of linen needed to supply a given number of Wacs for a year at an isolated post). Yours to solve are problems from the personnel, finance, procurement, supply, and medical departments.

If sewing is your skill, you can mend clothing, condition airplane wings, fold parachutes, and fill shoulder packs with food, medicine, weapons. You need a color sense and finger dexterity.

If the culinary department is your dish, you can prepare and cook food for women's meals (called mess).

If your manual ability takes larger dimensions, you can drive passenger cars, jeeps, forklift (not heavy) trucks, or tractors. Belinda D liked to work with her hands. She made her own clothes as soon as she was old enough, did weaving, and had a job with a couturière after college. A two-year stint in the Marines further developed her manual skills, for she learned to repair guns, oil equipment, change tires. On her release, she joined the Reserves, and supervised the weekly practice and competition of the Rifle and Pistol Team.

OFFICER QUALIFICATIONS. Training and experience, or study at officer candidate school after college are the ways to a commission. On graduation from OCS, you will be a second lieutenant Wac or Marine, or ensign WAVE. You may start training the summer before your senior year and be commissioned right after graduation. Officers must be resourceful, flexible, have good judgment, show leadership ability. WAVES must have 40/20 vision correctable to 20/20.

Besides the above, the Marine Corps demands at least an over-all C average; any major except pre-medicine, pre-dentistry, veterinary medicine, pharmacy, theology; that you be single until commissioned.

The Army requirements: age 21-28. Those with career experience may apply up to the age of 28 and be commissioned as first lieutenants. Officers are free to marry, may resign after two years of active duty.

Whatever the service you choose you may be assigned to one of a number of fields and can continue your postgraduate education toward technical or professional work.

IF YOU WANT TO WORK WITH PEOPLE, you can go into Personnel or Special Services.

The Personnel division greets recruits; keeps records of their education, experience, job preferences; evaluates their capabilities, assigns duties to them, keeps track of their performance, records their deeds and misdeeds. Officers interview, test, counsel, prepare reports, do job analysis, advise those returning to civilian life, teach.

Deborah L had always wanted to do personnel work. She majored in personnel administration at college, and went into the WAF after graduation. As second lieutenant, and then as first lieutenant, she counseled officer and enlisted personnel, described technical training courses, set up classifications, arranged transfers, and assigned officers who piloted and maintained jet bomber aircraft.

Special Services cover off-duty recreation. Experience with camp counseling, playgrounds, theatre groups, or the Scouts are good background. You supervise hobby shops, sports tournaments, find talent for theatricals, voices for glee clubs, arrange dances, set up swimming meets.

Judith D was born with theatre in her veins. In school she took part in every play she could; at college, she majored in dramatics and for her thesis designed the lighting, costumes, scenery of two plays, and directed them. In summer stock she was electrician, stage manager, actress. After graduation, when she joined the Marines, she became a member of the Recreation Council authorized to assign the funds spent on equipment.

If your interest in people is combined with training in a biological science, you may take advantage of openings for *electrocardiographers, nurses, pharmacists; X-ray, laboratory,* and *neuropsychiatric technicians, occupational* and *physical therapists, dental assistants*—and work with preventive medicine or with the ill and injured in hospitals and on shipboard. As an officer in the WAVES, Pauline V was the first woman to work in rehabilitation in a Naval hospital. She helped to set up the program, establish qualifications for its personnel, develop training procedures, and was one of the original people who used occupational therapy for technical training rather than as a time-killer during convalescence.

IF WORDS ARE YOUR MEDIUM, you can go into Information, Communications, or Intelligence.

Information is the section that tells the public and the military about plans, activities, and progress of military affairs —and provides opportunities for those who have been editors of their school paper, who have a feeling for language, an ability to communicate news by voice, word, or picture. This division conducts a public relations program through newspapers, books, magazines, radio, and TV.

Communications is the medium for keeping soldiers, sailors, tanks, and planes in touch all over the world. Those who go into it must have good coordination between mind, hand, ear; a memory for complicated codes; a clear voice; good hearing. The teletype machine and radio are their instruments. They learn the International Morse Code, send and receive messages; transmit pictures by radio photography; install, test, and maintain radio equipment, files, and ledgers; know rules about registered mail and money orders. Mrs. W, the wife of a book reviewer, worked in this division during the war, and reports that decoding taught her to watch for patterns; she still watches for them, but these days only to beat her husband at Scrabble.

Intelligence keeps officers informed. For it you need a foreign language to interpret broadcasts and translate news; you learn to read aerial photographs to find camouflaged bases; you piece together bits of conversation sent in from different parts of the world, uncover information about supplies and strategy.

IF YOU ARE INTERESTED IN NUMBERS, Logistics or Finance are open to you.

Logistics is the military term for the transportation and maintenance of men and materials. In this area, you learn to make requisitions, compute the expected length of time between ordering and receiving, take inventory, pack and send food and clothing. You write letters, keep supply information up to date, audit bills, watch warehouse stock and price changes, fill out forms, report gains or losses, sell surplus properties. You need to know the principles of classifying, marking, measuring, packing, storing.

Finance work deals with budgets, internal audits, statistical reports, pensions, prices of equipment, survivors' benefits, cost of transporting dependents.

IF YOU ARE SCIENTIFIC, Air Operations Support is one field for you. This department is charged with safe take-offs and landings of planes. Its ground specialists, observers, forecasters, equipment operators are trained in weather. One job is plotting weather data on charts, interpreting clouds, sending radio reports to observers, recording winds, working with balloons and meteorological instruments. The control tower operator tells incoming pilots what the visibility and ceiling height are and directs them to runways. Air Operations specialists and dispatchers assign passenger priorities. Aircraft Control and Warning operators locate the position and direction of aircraft, through radar. The Flight Traffic specialist is like an airline stewardess, but few women hold this job.

Other jobs include research on missile design or noise limens, requiring mathematics, physics, or chemistry; testing and repairing of electrical equipment; operation and installation of training devices; inspection and repair of timepieces, weapons, field glasses, gunsights.

IF YOU HAVE AN ART BACKGROUND, you might be interested in jobs concerned with linotype and monotype machines, binding, and making cost estimates; photographing for publicity, developing films, making prints, repairing cameras; drafting blueprints of buildings; making charts and maps; interpreting geographic data graphically, designing and lettering posters.

FOOD SERVICES furnish opportunities for *home economists*. They analyze menus; calculate nutrition and calorie content for a given age, sex, type of activity; oversee refrigeration, preparation of fresh, frozen, canned, dehydrated food; plan for large numbers far in advance.

IN THE LEGAL DEPARTMENT, *lawyers* study past and present laws related to military matters and policy guidance; review military court systems; work on contracts with foreign governments; or cope with legal problems that arise following accidents.

FOR THE MUSICAL are jobs as *choral directors* and *conductors* who manage bands, take part in civilian celebrations or television appearances.

GENERAL CONDITIONS

You get equal pay with men, free medical care, insurance, uniforms, meals and rent, or a cash allowance if you live off base. Vacations consist of 30 days' annual leave with pay; you can retire on half pay after 20 years, three-quarters pay after 30 years. Increases in pay and promotions are regular.

You can get special training and higher education, guidance about your abilities, your future, and your financial or family problems. Sports, dances, movies, libraries are provided for after-hours activity. On leave, you may use empty plane seats.

Those who elect the armed services are adaptable, self-assured, neither non-conformist nor escapist; lure of travel is not their motive. They feel a devotion to duty, enjoy routine and work to be done, and care about symbols and tradition.

For Further Information about Jobs or Training

Defense Advisory Committee on Women in the Services, The Pentagon, Washington 25, D.C.

VII

AUTOMATION

Fantasies out of Aladdin have become a reality through automation, a process that has brought conveniences, scientific advances, and jobs. Through it we can press a button and have dinner cooked for us, push a lever and get clothes laundered, use another to get our car out of the garage while we breakfast in bed. Doctors dial the telephone and in minutes learn from electronically kept records the uses and limitations of certain drugs; similarly lawyers can find out judgments handed down in previous lawsuits, without hours of research in several libraries.

Automation means getting things done automatically by electric power (not mechanical). Facts are organized into a special language and put into a machine that stores them (programming), and then gives them back when needed (processing).

It is not hard to understand: it happens every day in school. When you teach a child that one plus two equals three, you are programming. The next time he is given these two digits and responds with "three," he is processing. The language used is his language; nerve impulses enable him to receive the information, convey it to the brain for storage, and return it on request.

Data-processing machines (computers) are the focal point of automation. The range of their application is tremendous. In factories automobiles are assembled by machines which have the necessary instructions about order, timing, position, and what to do with defective parts. In science, sines, tangents, logarithms, and other algebraic data fed into a machine enable it to report what path a rocket would take if fired at a certain place, time, and speed. Problems that take men days and years are solved in seconds and hours.

Beginning jobs in this field fall naturally into two kinds: for the college graduate and for the high school graduate.

FOR THE COLLEGE GRADUATE

Programmer trainee is a starting job, leading to that of *computer* or *systems analyst* (sometimes called *programmer,* a term on the way out).

The computer analyst first learns how the business functions and decides if segments can be handled by a computer. If an airline wants a machine that will sell tickets directly to customers, the computer analyst will have to learn the details of how the airline takes orders for reservations, checks seating plans to avoid duplications, estimates price and tax, prints the tickets, and keeps notations of the transactions—steps hitherto taken by clerks using pencil, paper, telephone, charts, and time.

If the computer analyst decides the job can be handled by a computer, she makes the program for the machine's work. She first breaks down the job into separate steps, and writes the general block diagram which is the pictured flow of the solution.

On page 59 is a general block diagram for a simple operation.

Computers work on a yes-or-no system, which means with two possibilities for each instruction; therefore the computer analyst next makes a detailed block diagram which includes

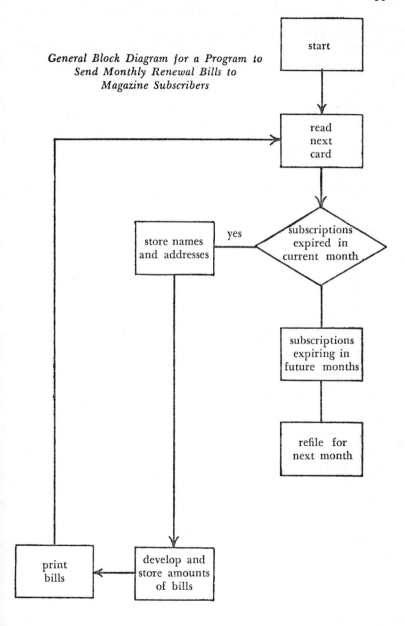

General Block Diagram for a Program to Send Monthly Renewal Bills to Magazine Subscribers

start

read next card

subscriptions expired in current month

store names and addresses — yes

subscriptions expiring in future months

refile for next month

develop and store amounts of bills

print bills

the development of the logic of the solution, the order in which operations must be performed, and a series of instructions broken down into small steps that allow single choices. There is often more than one route to the same answer; for instance, the shorter way to solve 9(102–12) is to do the subtraction first, then the multiplication; an automatic elevator is told to stop at floors in order of sequence, not in order of calls.

Next she translates facts and figures from the diagram into a language (code) the machine will accept, converts that into holes in cards or marks on tapes, feeds it to the machine for storage, and tests it.

The computer analyst is responsible for the entire process. Her tools are paper, pencil, eraser, template, and reference manuals. She may do the entire job herself, taking care of all the details, or may be assisted by a programming trainee who does such things as coding. Because of the complexity of different businesses, computer analysts usually specialize in one field (merchandising, public utilities, brokerage).

Advanced jobs are for those who design programs to be used in situations never met before. Charlotte Z has grown into such a job. She started as a programming trainee with a manufacturer of computing machines right after college, and then became a computer analyst. She worked at this job for seven years, taking on more and more intricate problems and proving her versatility and imagination. Today she works only in untried fields, devising programs for problems that have not yet been solved by automation. After all, there was a first time for the typewriter that produces English words from foreign dictation; the machine that takes instruction from handwritten numerals; the storing of measurements and rates of advertising media.

A *systems engineer* or *systems representative,* as she is called by the manufacturer of the machines, advises a company considering buying a machine as to which one will best serve the purpose—and whether they should buy one at all.

When a firm rents or buys a machine, a systems representative teaches the staff the detailing of the solution of the problems, and the use of the equipment. She may in time instruct new employees or customers of the manufacturing companies.

PERSONAL QUALITIES NEEDED. Those who have jobs dealing constantly with the public should be outgoing, attractive, honest, well-mannered, able to work with clerks and executives, free to travel. People drawn to this field are intelligent and human. They enjoy each other's company on and off the job, whether discussing problems or plays. The sometimes-expressed fear that they may become cold and mechanical is unfounded.

Many women who now hold executive positions began in a systems service department. One, who started as a representative, has become the employment manager in charge of the department which hires and places all employees, men and women, in her city. Another became head of the production department which designs, illustrates, and prints all instruction and promotional materials. One rose to a corporation vice presidency.

TRAINING NEEDED. College degrees are virtually required for programmers or systems analysts and representatives in the *scientific* field. The applicant must have a problem-solving or chess-playing type of mind and strong arithmetical and abstract reasoning ability. Those with mathematical knowledge deal with what-would-happen-if situations such as the effect of stresses in building a bridge, or with problems of cut and fill (dirt removal) in planning roads. Some companies want mathematicians; many of them get engineers and physicists; others accept those with mental prowess, whatever their major, as long as they have the ability to pass the aptitude test. All applicants must have a good command of English and be able to give lucid instructions orally and on paper. They start on a training program which lasts several weeks, and then are put on a job. They continue this training from time to time, as new and different machines are developed.

High school graduates, starting as operators, can sometimes advance to programmers and systems analysts on *business* problems after a number of years' experience.

Computer analysts depend on those who like to work with their hands. *Card punch machine operators* prepare the data to be put into the machine by punching holes on cards with a machine that works like a typewriter; the position of the holes represents different pieces of information. Sometimes the machines prepare perforated tapes instead of punched cards. The *verifying operator,* as the name implies, confirms the correctness of the work performed by the card punch machine operator; she uses a similar machine and inserts plungers through holes that are supposed to exist; if they don't a light goes on and she extracts the incorrect card. Some computers get instructions from magnetic tapes instead of punch cards.

A *console operator,* or *computer operator,* gets the equipment ready, sees that all necessary cards or tapes are there and in order, runs them through, keeps a run book (log of what she has done), and checks errors. Sometimes she operates auxiliary machines that translate the data back into words, numbers, or graphs which come out on narrow tapes or wide rolls of paper. A direction paper tape might, for example, be used in feeding a teletype wire—to send reports to branch offices from a central factory. The paper reports are used for lists, figures, or charts for people to work from directly.

A *tape librarian* has a basic knowledge of the terminology of the equipment, stores tapes between jobs, orders materials, gets out tapes when needed.

THE PROSPECTS

Jobs occur in companies that make the machines, in those that use them (for instance, banks, communications, factories, the government), and in centers which supply computing services for outside organizations on a fee basis (several hundred dollars an hour).

Machines range in size from a desk-size model to those several feet high and wide; they are clean (no leaking oil or ink). Hours are regular; offices are modern, brightly lighted, air conditioned. Starting salaries are considerably higher than in other fields and advance far and fast.

All hands are needed and that means women too. They are being recruited with men, though admittedly if two equally qualified people apply for the same job, and one of them is a man, he will probably be hired. Temporary setbacks in the economy can mean less interest in women, as it does elsewhere. But the total number of job openings is increasing, particularly for those at the design and planning level—clear evidence of the growing need for college-educated and technically trained personnel.

Automation is making it possible for us to have more hours in the day. It is manufacturing time, our most precious commodity. But we must use it wisely to get the most out of it. A $200,000 computer installed in a housing office made mistakes in 90 per cent of its answers during the first month because of wrong facts given to it; a census study reported that one county had more Britons than people. Machines cannot think, in the sense in which we use the term; they are subject to man. Man is subject to emotion. We can harness automation to our increasing advantage if we are Sorcerers, not Apprentices.

For Further Information about Jobs or Training

Association of Computing Machinery, 211 East 43rd Street, New York 17, New York

VIII

BOOKKEEPING AND ACCOUNTING

Bookkeeping is the systematic recording of financial affairs, and women are welcome in this job.

A *bookkeeper* works with systems, files, ledgers, journals, forms, paper work, comptometers, typewriters. She posts cash spent and amounts received; calculates pay checks taking into account the wages, hours worked, overtime, income-tax and social-security deductions, and withholdings for benefits; prepares bills, allowing for taxes, credits, amounts still due; makes out deposit slips, checks bank statements, verifies endorsements, makes corrections, balances books. In a small company her duties may be clerical, mechanical, and secretarial. In a large company she may handle only one phase such as the accounts receivable or payable, Christmas Club, classified ads.

The greatest demand is for machine operators because the field is rapidly taking advantage of the short cuts of automation. These operators must be quick and agile with their minds and their hands. Their job is to strike keys of calculating machines to put in the information, then press other keys to get the results—which might be customers' bills or whole payrolls. Some machine operators do this and nothing else, if the machines are intricate; others spend part of the time on office duties.

Responsible jobs, such as that of head bookkeeper or supervisor of the department, usually come through promotion, rather than through hiring from the outside.

PERSONAL QUALIFICATIONS. Methodical people who want things to be tidy enjoy this occupation. They are precise and thorough; if numbers don't add up they like taking pains to find out why. They enjoy the comfort of accuracy. They have the instinct that sees at once how a year can have 53 weeks from a payroll standpoint; they look for the meaning of a discrepancy before making a recalculation. High school is usually sufficient preparation, though some employers prefer junior college graduates.

Bookkeeping is a wide-open field for women. About a million workers were employed in it in 1960, three-quarters of whom were women, in every kind of organization.

Mrs. A showed how persistence and keeping up with the times could be lucrative in a shortage field. She was widowed at 25, with two children to support. She found a job as a bookkeeper, and began taking courses at night. She supported herself and her children, studied new machines and advance methods, and when her children went to college she was able to name her job and her salary because of her specialty.

ACCOUNTING

The *accountant* examines the work and methods of the bookkeeper, vouches for their accuracy and completeness, counts petty cash (the only money touched), prepares statements and final reports, and interprets them to the officers. An accountant is like a doctor, examining, diagnosing, and prescribing. The subject is the health of an organization's finances. Figures can never be as exact as coins. Values of inventories change with supply and demand; furniture and equipment depreciate with age; a business may show a profit but owe money. The accountant sees that the records are correct and the right conclusions drawn. His advance advice can prevent losses.

There are two kinds of accountants: the *private accountant* who works for a company on a salary basis; and the *certified public accountant* (CPA), who, either as an individual or member of a firm, works on a fee basis for outside organizations, corporations, non-profit offices, the government, or individuals such as doctors, actors, farmers, who are his clients. A company with no accountant on its staff, or one which prefers or is required to have an outside audit, turns to accounting firms for its periodic checkup.

CPAs have passed a certifying examination, required in many states; some public accountants do not take this examination, but may have to meet other local requirements.

GETTING STARTED IN ACCOUNTING.   The beginner, who may be a high school graduate, starts as a *bookkeeper, clerk, typist, stenographer, machine operator,* provided she has taken courses in mathematics, bookkeeping, commercial law, penmanship, stenography, typing. Some high schools provide additional training through interneship programs in which seniors may hold a job while still in school. The best place to start is a public accounting firm because it provides a variety of experience. College graduates are eligible for the CPA examination after two years' apprenticeship; some states require that their major be accounting.

Clerks might add figures for bank deposits, count typewriters for an inventory, total payroll cards for a timekeeper, or calculate salary deductions. *Typists* and *secretaries* write covering letters for reports, type results of audits, file correspondence, answer the telephone, mail statements.

THE JOB IS NOT JUST ARITHMETICAL.   Accountants watch for patterns, for inconsistencies within these patterns (why were withdrawals heavy one month or the bank charges higher than usual?), keep their eye out for tax advantages the firm may not be aware of (a fire damage that may be deductible) or for a method of reducing expenses (perhaps by allocating some bills to another year). They watch to see that profits are real: hidden expenses like telephone calls and postage may not have been considered. In a new business they install the accounting system and teach it to the employees.

QUALIFICATIONS. Accountants need a sleuthing type of mind, complete understanding of what figures are saying, ability to make order out of a raft of details, to write, do research, and work under pressure. Those who like constant change from one topic to another and who work well with people will enjoy public accounting. They will have to explain or correct errors or listen to the personal problems of a staff delighted at finding a new ear. This field presents a challenge to those who like to search without knowing what they are looking for until they find it, can examine evidence, draw conclusions.

SPECIALTIES WITHIN AND WITHOUT THE FIELD. You may prefer to teach accounting, thereby getting a chance to deal with people as well as numbers. Or, if you want to write, you can prepare explanatory reports for those who have difficulty reading budgets or who find the cash basis easier than the accrual. You can apply accounting to a particular business, such as restaurants, retailing, employment. If your interest is accounting itself, you can specialize: a budget accountant watches to see that departments stay within their budgets; a cost accountant determines the true cost of goods, services, labor, materials, overhead; a tax accountant, sometimes with additional courses in law, studies the effects of new regulations. Or accounting may be background for another profession. Some men and women, heads of trade associations, or in politics, education, and the government, are trained accountants.

CAREER OPPORTUNITIES. At the top of the scale, titles are

public accountant, private accountant (or *executive, administrative, industrial, general, chief accountant*), *controller* (usually spelled correctly in this field), *actuary, auditor, bookkeeper, budget officer, cashier, credit manager, office manager, purchasing agent, sales analyst, statistician, fiscal officer, treasurer.*

Beginning salaries compare well with those in other fields. College graduates, with accounting majors, earn the most. At the top of the scale, professional accountants earn as much as doctors, dentists, lawyers, and engineers.

The future is good. More people will be needed as government regulations make problems more complicated. The need for those who can plan systems and make use of the new machines is becoming intense. In 1961 there were 400,000 accountants and auditors in the United States, including 70,000 CPAs.

CAREER DRAWBACKS. The work can be hard and tedious; the surroundings may range from a carpeted office to a drafty warehouse. Travel is often involved, and overtime when tax returns are due. There is opposition to women by some clients. Only about 10 per cent of all accountants and 2 per cent of all CPAs are women.

This field does hold out opportunities, though, for women who can do the work and take the difficulties. They have been successful as staff accountants and in their own business; they have been teachers, without the hazard of overtime. Chances for part-time jobs are good because of the need for periodic checkups and quarterly work, and these provide a way to keep in touch with the field during marriage.

For Further Information about Jobs or Training

American Institute of Certified Public Accountants, 270 Madison Avenue, New York 16, New York

Controllers Institute of America, 2 Park Avenue, New York 16, New York

National Association and Council of Business Schools, 601–13th Street, N.W., Washington 5, D.C.

The American Woman's Society of Certified Public Accountants, 237 South LaSalle Street, Chicago 4, Illinois

The Institute of Internal Auditors, 120 Wall Street, New York 5, New York

IX

FASHION AND RETAILING

FASHION

Most women are interested in fashion. As children they dress
their dolls; as growing girls they dress themselves; as mothers
they dress their daughters.

When they decide they want to get paid for their interest
they have one of a number of things in mind. Some would
like to live with a pencil in one hand and a drawing pad in
the other, dream up new styles, and see their sketches come
true. Some would rather deal with the people who turn the
sketch into reality and onto the customer. Some want to work
behind the scenes and talk about fashion.

GETTING STARTED.   In general, there are two ways in, whatever the final goal. One is to work with the materials that
make up clothes; the other is to work on paper and describe
them.

Working with the materials means working with the stuff
of the trade, which is important in the end anyway. To understand the possibilities of a design and the way it will look
in three dimensions, you have to know how different fabrics
act: which are stiff, which pliable, how they fold, how they
are best used. And you must know how a pin or buckle will

look *on* a dress rather than just by itself; which colors go with what and when and where—summer or winter, Boston or Phoenix.

One of the ways to learn is in manufacturers' showrooms, often called Seventh Avenue, after the famous street in New York, where most of them are. These are in effect stores run by the makers and designers of the clothes; their customers are those who buy for retail stores. An *apprentice* helps out all around; she runs errands, picks up pins, drapes designs on dummies. A *colorist* (with art and textile training) fills in designers' sketches to get the total effect; an *assistant designer* (with an A.B. in dress design or design-school training) selects fabrics, does cutting, sketches ideas, translates designers' drawings into the finished product. *Sales clerks* show dresses, hats, coats to buyers and the press, arrange displays, do office work, model the clothes, sew hems and buttons. A *follow-up girl* checks on shipments.

Retail stores also have openings for beginning sales clerks. Besides selling, these clerks count inventory, see that stock is correctly ticketed, put it away; they know their merchandise, suggest substitutes to customers, keep displays in order, answer questions about corresponding sizes or the care of a dress, write sales slips, operate cash registers, process charge plates, wrap packages, look into purchases not received, take care of exchanges.

Pattern companies hire beginners who can sew to make up samples of trimmings that show how they can be used with different styles.

If you have the figure, which means the required dimensions, not just good proportions, you can be a *model* for a manufacturer, store, magazine. It is exhausting to your patience and your bones: means lunch en route between appointments; long waiting for your turn; then holding a pose while photographer, stylist, and assistants pin a sleeve here, or hem there, finally discard the finished picture and make you do it all over again. You may model a cocktail dress in a comfortable air-conditioned studio, a bathing suit on a windy sailboat, or a fur coat in the hot summer sun.

The way in through paper work is for *secretaries*. On women's magazines they schedule fashion shows, line up models, telephone those who fail to appear, supply coffee, arrange a dress for the background of a story for a before-and-after situation, or to feature the fashion-of-the-month. In pattern departments they help write directions, interpret them, answer inquiries from the public. In advertising agencies they work for copywriters, either on a fashion account or in the department which provides props and accessories for the copy of accounts such as automobiles, cigarettes, cruises.

Let's see where you can go from here.

DO YOU WANT TO DRAW?   The epitome is, of course, the *fashion designer* (or *stylist*) who has or finds ideas that prompt new styles. She must have an art and textile background. She keeps ahead of the latest trends, travels here and abroad, observes what styles catch on, or don't. She prepares patterns, sketches the outline on printed forms, draws various parts to full scale, cuts out drawings to make experimental patterns, writes specifications which must include color, measurements, kind of material. She uses rulers, drawing instruments, scissors. She needs the skill to sketch the human figure, imagination to visualize the finished product, a color sense, ability to wear clothes well herself, knowledge of fabrics and of the technique of making garments so as to instruct cutters, fitters, sewers.

DO YOU WANT TO HELP SET FASHION?   A *buyer* is the focal point of the fashion business. She is the person who decides what stock to lay in, how much, and when. She must be a Nostradamus. Here is where ingenuity, fast thinking, frantic activity, and stiff competition come in. The buyer keeps ahead of the public, knows the coming fashion, stocks it, decides on price, sees that it moves. She must be a good judge of the probable lifetime of a color, a low-belted dress, high-vamped shoe. In her work it is always June in January; she plans her stock months in advance.

Her guess must be close to reality; she cannot afford to make mistakes and end up with a large supply she can't sell. If the skirted bathing suits are left over in September, she is stuck with them; they won't sell in October, and by next summer two-piece suits may be the fashion. She makes an educated guess and buys realistically, going on many past records: types of merchandise, sizes, color appeal. The merchandise market helps her, and she spends at least a quarter of her time there. She bargains with the manufacturer, notes costs, tries to keep them down. She knows what her customers' pocketbooks will bear.

In a retail store the consumers are the public; in a resident buying office the customers are affiliated stores across the country which count on the buyers to tell them what to order. A resident buyer does not need promotional ability—her customers are built in; but she does need to know local idiosyncrasies (gold shoes sell in the South, not in New York).

Harriet F proves how far-reaching a buyer's influence can be, and how varied the job. As a free-lance merchandise adviser she helps out-of-town buyers. She does a great deal of research first, visits manufacturers and designers, collects pages of notes about fashions and accessories, travels to the stores themselves, holds briefings with the buyers, keeps up with personnel changes that may affect a store's thinking. Then, in person and through a monthly publication, she suggests not only styles but methods of display, advertising, and marketing. She developed this job herself after 40 years in the field. Her first salaried job was advertising copywriter with a store; her last was vice president of an expensive dress shop in New York.

The *fashion coordinator* assists the buyers. She is responsible for seeing that all hands are kept up to date. Her role is to advise buyers, help the advertising writers, set up fashion shows, train models, assemble furniture for window displays, arrange sample rooms. In a fabric house, as *fashion firm co-ordinator,* her job is to arrange shows for buyers and for the press.

The person who likes the challenge of many kinds of people and demands, the job of getting them all to pull together, will enjoy fashion coordinating. She must have a talent for decorating and display.

A *comparison shopper* keeps buyers informed of the prices and quality of comparable goods sold by other stores. Sometimes posing as a customer, sometimes quite openly, she visits stores, writes up their stock, perhaps buys it to take away for closer inspection. Or she may work for a fiber company as market liaison, visit manufacturers' showrooms to see how the company's materials are being used, and suggest other ways of using them. (A new insulating fabric might be made up into parkas by one manufacturer who never thought of it for linings.)

DO YOU WANT TO WRITE? Services concerned with informing the trade and public about what is going on are places for those who want to tell the story of fashion, not produce it. They are women's magazines, fashion publications, house organs, trade journals, newspapers.

On a magazine the *fashion editor* may sketch her ideas for a coat to be featured or may spend all her time in the manufacturers' salesrooms keeping up to date, never putting pen to paper; the *designer* works out the details of the coat; the *stylist* (or *picture stylist*) decides on the background (a baseball field, restaurant, or city street), the *accessories editor* chooses jewelry, gloves, hat, shoes; the *photographer* sets the scene, decides on lighting, chooses the pose, takes the picture.

An *advertising copywriter* composes copy for newspapers, flyers, promotion pamphlets. She spends almost as much time getting the facts as she does writing. She may have a job with an agency or in the advertising department of a store.

Reporters on magazines and newspapers write up the news about styles or people in the field.

A FUTURE IN FASHION. New York is the hub of the fashion industry in this country. California holds second place. Other fashion centers are Portland (Oregon), St. Louis, Minneapolis, Chicago, Dallas, Milwaukee, Cleveland, Kansas City. Most of the resident buying offices are in New York; a few are in Chicago and Los Angeles.

The pace is fast, competitive: the point is to get there first. Working conditions vary: they may be noisy and untidy; sometimes (in expensive salons) serene and orderly. Beginning salaries are low. Fashion designers on the way up may earn good salaries, but they may find themselves expendable: job security is slim. Models can earn enormous amounts per hour, but every hour may not be filled.

Those aiming for the top may be either high school or college graduates. It is a field for women, and if they can take it, nothing can hold them back.

RETAILING

We have been looking at the fashion end of retailing. But retailing is more than fashion.

Retailing is a field that has everything—for the customer and for the job hunter. A department store is a small city. You can buy a hat, get a meal, store your furs, mail a letter, park your child, book a tour, or get someone else to do it all for you.

Retailing is a part of the process of getting products to customers, and there are many aspects to it besides buying and selling. One of the greatest of *non sequiturs* is "I don't want to go into retailing because I don't like to sell."

The work of the retail business is generally divided into five divisions, although the exact setup varies from store to store: merchandising, personnel, sales promotion, financial control, store operations.

MERCHANDISING. Most women who go into the merchandising division start by selling. They must have selling experience for advancement, but a few months is sufficient. Besides, selling experience is good training for any other field.

The next step up may be *section manager,* sometimes called *divisional selling superintendent* or *service manager.* Her duties are supervisory. She oversees the sales clerks, is responsible for sales techniques, takes care of complaints and adjustments. The next promotion is to *junior assistant buyer,* or *assistant buyer,* and then to *buyer.* This progression has a number of variations. Some people jump over the intervening steps and become buyers; others may assist first in small departments and then major ones before becoming buyers.

Some beginners start as *stock clerks.* This job entails putting stock away when it comes from the warehouse or manufacturer, getting it out on call, and sending it to the departments that need it. The *head of stock* may come up from stock clerk or from selling. She is in charge of the clerks, sees that sufficient merchandise is on hand throughout the store for the sales and for display, reports when more should be ordered.

PERSONNEL. You can get into this division through selling or office work. This division hires, trains, lays off, terminates employees; administers the wage and salary program and such employees' services as the house organ, recreation, cafeteria, medical care, and counseling.

Amelia B became a receptionist in the personnel department of a Philadelphia store, after getting her A.B. in English. She learned to screen applicants, estimate qualifications, and work with store personnel. Within a year she was promoted to interviewer, and four months later became employment director, responsible for the placement, transfer, and promotion of 2,600 employees at all levels of jobs, besides 1,000 seasonal sales clerks.

SALES PROMOTION. This division includes advertising, art work, copywriting, production, display, special events. One of the duties here is seeing to it that the mail-order telephone clerks always have copies of today's newspaper ads, so they will be familiar with the goods ordered, and also be able to suggest the featured buy of the day. Beginners can start as *writers* if they have had writing or journalism courses and can learn to produce good copy. *Artists* lay out ads, design shopping bags or posters, choose type faces for store directories.

Theodora P majored in art in college, and got a job as layout artist for a store in her college town. She showed unusual ability in knowing how to present merchandise attractively and honestly. Two years later she became the advertising manager, and her work became known in both trade and consumer publications. A leading specialty store in Boston noticed her and in less than a year asked her to take over its advertising department. A quick rise in a short time.

FINANCIAL CONTROL. Bookkeeping, accounting, charge-account authorization, bill adjustments, credit, come under this department. *Bookkeeping clerk* is the way in, and the training needed for advancement includes experience plus the educational requirements for financial work.

STORE OPERATIONS. Housekeeping functions occupy this division: the receiving and marking of merchandise from the warehouse; delivery to customers; information; personal shopping service; adjustments; repair and alterations; building maintenance; protection.

WHERE THE JOBS ARE. Department stores, suburban branches, mail-order houses, resident buying offices, specialty shops, retail training schools, and merchandising associations are sources of openings. Agnes S combined an interest in people with experience in retailing. She spent her undergraduate summers selling, taught school for two years after college, then with this background became head of admissions for a school of fashion design.

Retail stores handle everything imaginable, but those with good prospects for women include books, candy, clothes, cosmetics, gifts, jewelry, novelties, toys.

EDUCATIONAL REQUIREMENTS. High school graduates can start in merchandising as sales or stock clerks. But college training is becoming so important that in large stores and some chains it is almost essential for advancement today. College graduates join an executive training squad and alternate between classroom work and selling, rotating from department to department (to learn the difference involved in selling lingerie and hardware). In class the theory and techniques of the business are taught by store executives and leaders in the field. Length of training varies with the store and its needs, but is usually under a year. A number of stores like to hire college juniors for the college shops during August, hoping to interest them in a permanent job after graduation.

Some stores have highly organized training programs; others are less formal and the progress not as clearly defined; a few, which have a good deal of self-service, start trainees as supervisors' assistants instead of in sales.

You must have a real interest in people; a competitive mind—which means you are eager to beat last year's sales figures and want to do something about it if you don't; ability to add and subtract, calculate percentages, run around a lot, follow directions, do several things at once, work under pressure, and take long hours and many days (weekends may turn into workdays except in resident buying offices; hours are normal there). If you also have administrative ability and want to get ahead, the sky's the limit.

Beginning salaries are apt to be low, but rise quickly and go very high. Purchase discounts, commissions, and bonuses add more.

OPENINGS. Two things are happening in the retail field which are causing a shift in jobs. One is the growth of shopping centers and suburban stores, bringing good opportunities outside of big cities (usually only in merchandising; the other divisions often operate from the main store). The other is the increased use of automation, which reduces sales and clerical openings.

Retailing is the third largest business in the United States, growing with the population and the rising standard of living. And it is a made-to-order field for women. They can have part-time jobs, either part of the day, or on Saturdays plus the evenings the store is open; they can get temporary jobs before Christmas and in the summer. They can enter retailing after being away from a job; set up their own shop in their home town; or run large stores in big cities.

After college Flora N went on the stage and had a number of acting jobs until she married. During her married years in San Francisco she appeared on radio and television from time to time. When her children were in their teens she got a selling job with a dress shop, developed into a stylist, and fifteen years later opened up her own store. The theatre had given her a background in human behavior, costume design, and make-up which were effectively applied to retailing. She was successful in her own business not only locally but with clients who came to her from as far away as New York because she was always understanding and up to date.

The retail field has had women at the very top, and still has room for more. For many years the president of a prominent New York specialty store was a woman. Another writes a daily newspaper column of fashion advice that is followed nationally. Another founded and directs a well-known school of fashion design.

If beginners, returners, older women, and those changing over from another field have what it takes, they will find this door wide open.

For Further Information about Jobs or Training

National Retail Merchants Association, 100 West 31st Street, New York 1, New York

X

FINANCE

"Women advance in finance in spite of us, not because of us," a bank vice president once said. Before we get too feministic, let's admit that women themselves are partly responsible for prejudice. "I never *could* balance my checkbook" is a familiar phrase, and yet women are as quick as the next man to catch someone shortchanging them. Besides, some women have managed to become bank presidents, vice presidents, trust officers, managers, bank directors, and bank owners. The Treasurer of the United States is a woman, and all paper currency carries her signature. And so those still undecided about their careers should not reject this field automatically.

Finance is the management of the flow of money.

Everyone is interested in money: the child with her piggy bank, the miser and his piles of gold, the young adult starting life on a shoestring, and the wealthy financier. Even those with incomes in six figures watch expenses. Some, for instance, pay tuitions in installments through a special plan, for income advantage. Yet many people think that *jobs* concerned with money must be dull. An understanding of the almost limitless facets of finance should dispel this notion.

BANKING

Banks are one of several services needed to take care of the flow of money. They store our cash, enable us to get it or pay bills quickly and safely by check, put the money to work by lending it.

As customers we deal chiefly with the *teller*. She verifies signatures, cashes checks, sees that deposit slips are added correctly, counts change quickly, must be accurate, unruffled, and, as the customers' main contact, courteous.

You may think her day starts at nine o'clock and stops at three—bankers' hours. But that's a misnomer. Many other activities take place to make the dealings smooth.

Before the bank opens in the morning, the teller gets her cash from the vault, counts it, sends for more if she needs it. After the bank closes to you, she sorts checks and deposit slips, files cards of new accounts, removes those of closed accounts, counts cash, balances her day's accounts.

Fourteen billion checks are handled by banks in this country every year. These checks are processed behind the scenes where two-thirds of all bank employees are, as are also many starting jobs.

Clerks cancel, file, and sort checks, add and record the amounts; they collect deposit slips, get information on customers' balances, prepare and mail statements, gather checks drawn on other banks and arrange for their clearance. Some of this work is done by hand, much by machine.

The career-minded clerk can study the operations of a bank, become familiar with customers' accounts, names, and signatures, learn to see that enough money is in the accounts to cover the checks, and return checks when payment is stopped.

Commercial banks and trust companies (where we have our checking accounts) and some savings banks rent safe deposit boxes; lend money; settle estates, file wills, collect insurance, arrange for distribution of property, serve as guardians of minors; analyze, purchase, and sell securities for customers and keep track of their holdings; and sometimes have foreign accounts (finance the importing and exporting of goods, maintain accounts of depositors in other countries, issue traveler's checks and letters of credit).

Part of the money is lent to individuals for varying lengths of time, at interest (enabling them to build a house, buy a car, pay for an education); part is invested in other businesses (enabling them to buy equipment, increase staffs, or build factories).

Many departments take care of these operations. All have clerical assistants; all are in the charge of officers. Here *clerks* prepare charges for services performed, keep records of loans made and securities held, notify officers of cash on hand and amounts to be kept on reserve for depositors, interview applicants for loans, check credit and references, attend safe deposit vaults, identify boxholders, and keep records of their visits.

For those who want to get ahead in banking, such jobs can lead anywhere.

NON-BANKING JOBS IN BANKS.   Depending on the size of the bank, there may be *correspondents, librarians, nurses, personnel officers, publicity writers, restaurant managers, training directors, translators, welfare workers.* Professional specialists are *accountants, economists, engineers, lawyers, statisticians,* who study, advise, and write reports on companies seeking loans. And many banks have women's departments where women depositors may deal with a woman.

OFFICERS.   Most banks have at least three kinds: *president* (in charge of the entire operation); one or more *vice presidents* (serving as general managers or in charge of a department); *comptroller*—the misspelling from an early error still in use—sometimes called *cashier*. Small banks may be managed entirely by these officers. Large banks also have *assistant officers* in the trust, credit, investment departments.

There were 115,000 bank officers in the United States in 1960, one-tenth of whom were women, those mostly assistant cashiers. Banking employs more women than any other field of finance.

The quickest advancement is usually in a large city bank where you can start on the training program, and learn by moving from one department to another, doing clerical work in each. Or you can start in the stenographic pool, another chance to get a bird's-eye view. In a small bank you begin in a clerical job and work up through experience and outside courses.

WHAT KIND OF EDUCATION DO YOU NEED? A high school diploma is enough to get you started, but you should have taken some business education courses such as bookkeeping, business arithmetic, typing, stenography. Advancement is helped by a college background, but depends on further education in any case. The American Institute of Banking has courses for employees of member banks. Local banking associations sponsor other schools.

WHAT KIND OF WOMAN MAKES A GOOD BANKER? First, strangely enough, you don't have to be a mathematical whiz. In fact, if you are, you will probably hate banking; certainly steer clear if theoretical math is your bent (unless you go into the tabulating department and work with computers and other business machines—an area with great opportunities). You do have to be able to make change easily, understand numbers, calculate percentages or interest rates quickly.

You should be honest, decisive, courageous, understanding, accurate, able to grasp unfamiliar problems, get along with people, have a good memory, and be discreet because banks know so much of people's private affairs (the reassuring sound of silence, as one bank puts it). It is a business for the well balanced who can cope both with routine work and work requiring initiative. If you are artistic, restless, or if you like a frantic pace, it is not for you.

OUTLOOK. Employment is steadier than in many other fields because banks are little affected by layoffs or slow business. Even when banks merge, they keep open; if they have to cut down on personnel, they do so by not replacing those who leave or retire. Advancement is steady, not meteoric; opportunities to earn high salaries do exist; and as a group, banks offer more fringe benefits than any other industry. The surroundings are clean, well lighted, and air conditioned. The work is seldom strenuous.

Banks are everywhere, in large cities and small towns. New York, California, Pennsylvania, and Illinois hire about one-third of all employees of commercial banks.

BROKERAGE

When a company needs money to expand its services or build a warehouse, it gets it by selling stocks (shares in a company) or bonds (loans made to a company). The sales of stocks or bonds are handled by brokers or a brokerage business.

Stocks are bought and sold on the stock exchange as in an auction. There are stock exchanges in most cities in the country and branches in other cities. Trading on the exchange, because it is considered fast and rough, is the only job in finance barred to women. If a woman inherits a membership (called a seat) that lets one trade on the exchange, she must sell it.

Aside from the beginning job of *secretary*, beginners might start as *clerks*, who count proxies, sort coupons, chalk up quotations from the ticker tape in offices that don't have electric boards for recording stock prices.

A SECTION OF TICKER TAPE [1]

GMP	X	DD
pf		
5s84½	2s45 1/8	191

---

[1] This tape reports:

500 shares of General Motors (GMP) preferred stock sold at $84.50.

pf below the symbol indicates preferred stock.

5s before the price stands for 500 shares; the number of shares is expressed in hundreds by a digit and an s.

200 shares of U.S. Steel (X) sold at $45.12½.

100 shares of E. I. DuPont de Nemours (DD) sold at $191.

if the number of shares is 100 the price stands alone.

Junior analysts seek figures and facts about products; add earnings, sales, and the effect of price changes or of competing products; draw graphs of trends in certain industries; write summaries. They begin on training courses in large brokerage firms and the research departments of banks. They may

SECTION OF NEWSPAPER REPORT
OF NEW YORK STOCK EXCHANGE TRANSACTION [2]

Current Year			1st	H	L	Net Last Change
H	L					
41¼	26	Int Silver 1.10b	33	33¼	32⅝	32⅝ —
19½	12½	Del & Hud .60e	16	16	15¼	15¾ −¼
194¾	105¼	Corning G 1.50a	155¼	156½	151½	151⅝ 22⅝
58½	33	Int Tel & Tel 1xd	41⅝	41¾	40¾	40¾ −⅞

[2] At the left of the stock name are the highest and lowest prices at which the stock sold this year. The right columns show yesterday's first, highest, lowest, and last sales prices, and the net change from the preceding day.

The symbols after the stock names relate to dividends.

The above list tells:

International Silver pays a dividend of $1.10 per year plus some dividends in the form of stock.

Delaware and Hudson has paid 60¢ so far this year.

Corning Glass pays $1.50 a year plus some extra dividends.

International Telephone and Telegraph pays $1 per year, but if you buy this stock today you will not be eligible for a dividend until the next one declared.

keep up to date the lists of clients' holdings (portfolios); answer telephone questions about current bid and asked prices of stocks; draw up reports about companies' financial standing for brokers; record orders from customers to buy or sell stock. They learn to examine financial records and physical plants, and make and record sales. Their tools are rulers, colored pencils, charts, quotations in small type.

A junior analyst may advance to the position of *broker,* also known as *registered representative,* a person who buys and sells stocks and bonds; *security analyst,* sometimes called *statistician* or *researcher,* who studies the corporation represented by the stock or bond and passes on the findings to the broker, who uses them as the basis of the advice he gives prospective buyers; *portfolio analyst,* who sets up the investment plans of clients, taking into consideration their objectives—capital gain or regular income, for example.

To get ahead you should be a college graduate with a major in economics, have an aptitude for figures, get along with people, be a good salesman, and have good hearing because much of the buying and selling is done by telephone.

Brokerage employs the second largest number of women in finance.

INVESTMENT BANKING

Investment banking differs from other banking in many respects: it provides the money for a company (underwrites the loan) before putting its bonds or stock on the market; it is generally concerned only with long-term investments; it does no personal or commercial banking.

Beginners who have specialized in corporate finance, economics, or accounting start in the buying department and work with the investigators who tour the factories; they learn to read balance sheets and mortgage maps, and use adding machines and reference books. Needed in the long run are engineers, lawyers, patent experts to study technical aspects of a business. The selection of issues to be underwritten is done by partners or officers. Very few opportunities are available to women in investment banking.

INVESTMENT COUNSELING

Investment counselors advise on the management of investments. There are two kinds: counselors who maintain a subscription service that issues recommendations (the same advice going to all subscribers); the investment counsel firm which manages the funds of individual clients.

Researchers and *statisticians* produce the background information; *supervisors* oversee customers' investments, constantly advising on what steps to take.

Although still small, investment counseling has grown faster than any other division of the industry. It is a big-city occupation, but beginning experience may be gained in any bank, brokerage house, or bond firm. Opportunities for women are distinctly limited, and yet if they have the ability nothing holds them back.

Mrs. N went to work for an investment counseling firm right from college. After ten years she left to get married, having achieved the status of counselor. Interested in the subject, she continued to manage her own investments while raising a family. She even undertook things usually beyond the reach of women and which keep them out of this field. She examined bridge construction and went through mines to check on the observance of safety rules and the quality of the products. Eighteen years later she had been so successful because of her thorough investigations and her ability to make wise decisions uninfluenced by others (considered a special feat in this business) that she was offered a partnership in an investment firm.

MUTUAL FUNDS

Mutual funds or investment companies invest clients' money in securities and give in return shares in the mutual fund. These companies maintain their own portfolio through the use of shareholders' money, which they manage for a fee. Individual investors may buy shares on the installment plan or invest in lump sums.

There are two kinds of investment companies: the closed end, in which there is a fixed amount to invest, and after that no more shares for sale; and the open end, in which shares are always for sale.

Investment decisions are made by the directors, but mature women with the sales ability and imagination to find new prospects are sought for this field: the whole graduating class of a university was persuaded by a saleswoman to use a mutual fund to save for its 25th reunion gift.

For Further Information about Jobs or Training

Association of Stock Exchange Firms, 24 Broad Street, New York 5, New York

Investment Counsel Association of America, Inc., 100 Park Avenue, New York 16, New York

New York Stock Exchange, 11 Wall Street, New York 5, New York

The American Bankers Association, 12 East 36th Street, New York 16, New York

XI

FREE-LANCE

THE PROS AND CONS. Free-lance work is the envy of many nine-to-fivers, but it is not the independent, unpressured, hedonistic existence it seems to be from the outside.

A free-lancer works on her own time, which can mean 24 hours a day, and on her own responsibility.

Such work seems attractive because of its freedom from time clock, supervisor, sometimes office walls. But free-lancers often have to play games with themselves to turn out work. Bertha N goes to magazine editors to ask them to consider an article she has written; when she finds interest she goes home and writes it; without that needle she cannot knuckle down. Others feel the irregularity of income is worrisome. The fact that many who do this kind of work are creative adds another hazard, the variableness of inspiration.

There are advantages, especially to women with home commitments, to those who want to earn extra cash only now and then, and to those who seek variety. If you have the necessary self-discipline as well as the ability to do the job, it has much in its favor.

BEFORE YOU BEGIN FREE-LANCING. Get experience in a full-time capacity—especially if you need a living wage. You can, however, start at once to build assignments on the side, if you have time and energy after a regular job. Take whatever comes along, even if it is not quite what you want to do in the end.

YOUR OWN BUSINESS

If you want to establish your own business, the way you proceed will determine your ultimate success as much as your ability does. If you have such a poor head for bookkeeping, legal terms, insurance regulations and taxes that you close your eyes and pretend they aren't there, then get a partner who can keep his open! You cannot do business and be un-businesslike. Doris E, a service-minded person, opened an agency for nurses. She sent out announcements, advertised for applicants, and got calls from hospitals, clinics, schools, patients, nurses, and soon had a thriving business. One day, when she had a question about filling out a tax form, she called her lawyer; he asked her to come to see him. After an hour's consultation, he said she had broken 19 laws (had not checked references, given introduction cards to nurses or receipts for fees paid). He straightened her out just in time to avoid inconveniences and penalties.

The Small Business Administration in Washington publishes booklets about permits, licenses, laws, records (you can't just list income and expenses in your own fashion: there are regulations about the form); insurance (you must carry unemployment insurance for anyone you hire); financing the business; making a budget; choosing the business site; the relative merits of a partnership *vs.* a corporation. Some states have a program to show you how to market a product, set prices, determine local needs. Find out from the Chamber of Commerce if your state has one.

In short, it is not simply a matter of being able to make a gadget apron that your friends love or hotcakes that sell like hotcakes in winter.

HOME WORK

If you don't want to budge from the house, think about editing, writing, or commercial art if you have ability along one of those lines. Take your work to publishers and get your name on their files. If you can't go to them, send samples of your writing, photographs of your art, a sheet of your experience. *Why Not Write* lists publications and the kinds of subjects they print. You might try book reviewing by sending reviews to newspapers and magazines; they may print them and pay nothing at first, but if you continue and are successful, they may send you books to review, as well as checks.

Other possibilities include correcting school papers, tutoring, or giving lessons in painting, piano, remedial reading, or other subjects.

In a number of instances, groups of women with experience in the writing field have joined forces and set up editorial services, each member of the team having a different specialty: copy editing, proofreading, rewriting, translating. Some are free-lancing only; others are combining their assignments with full-time jobs. They got started through the help of former employers or good promotion flyers; after that they were under way in a business whose volume they could control according to their own schedules.

Designing greeting cards is a sure way of getting a start in free-lance art if you can produce something different and in line with what a particular company wants. Study the cards put out by various companies to learn their style. This procedure proved to be a lifesaver for Albertha V after she had been in a mental hospital for six years. She was going to be discharged, and her doctor wanted her to earn some money before she left, so that she could gain confidence for the permanent job she would look for. She visited a number of greeting card manufacturers, showed them samples of her work, and on the first day had an order for 50 cards from one of them.

Then, too, you may have money in your hands if you are good at cooking, sewing, photography, picture framing, typing, bookkeeping. Or you might become a telephone message-taker either by letting your clients give your number or by having a line connected from their telephone to yours. Or you might tell neighborhood stores you will advertise today's specials by telephone, if you get a commission from resulting sales. Many more ideas can be found in *How To Earn an Income Selling Products and Services by Phone.*

See if a clipping bureau will catch on; read many newspapers, cut out news about local citizens, and send it to them on the chance that they might engage you to do this regularly.

The key is fitting your skills to current needs.

Delia T, who had been working in England as an advertising copywriter, returned to Boston when business fell off. She found it difficult to get a job because she was 65. Employers told her they could not put her on their retirement plan; the fact that she was willing to waive retirement benefits made no difference. She decided to use her office skills and set up a secretarial service. All she needed was one assignment. A philanthropist's wife asked her to come in three mornings a week to balance her checkbook, write letters, make up seating lists for dinners. She did so well that a similar job came along from the daughter-in-law, and that job led to others, including arranging private libraries, proofreading, preparing manuscripts. Within a year she was turning business away; at 75 she is still going.

Some women are notary publics (officials who witness signatures, give oaths, take written testimony). You must be a U.S. citizen, resident of the state you work in, licensed, take the oath of office. You are paid by clients' fees.

Manufacturing novelties can sometimes be started at home, but may have to be moved if the output becomes too large.

Original games catch on if they are different. Nellie F and her husband invented a vocabulary card game; they were able to clear space in the basement and make these themselves; but after department stores started to order them, rented space and assistants were required.

You might start a mail-order business of items already on the market. Carry products that will bring re-orders or are related; in other words, don't sell just fire screens: there won't be many demands from one household or repeat orders, since screens don't wear out.

Check the zoning laws. One summer two high school girls in a town in Pennsylvania wanted to earn money for college. They set up a baby-sitting service, a seemingly lawful enterprise, at one of their houses, but a neighbor told them it was illegal to do business in a residential section. They applied to the zoning board for approval but their application was rejected.

AWAY FROM HOME

If you want to be on the go and around town, you might be an insurance agent, real estate saleswoman, market research interviewer, nurse, oral book reviewer (retelling a story for women's clubs), organizer of children's parties (if you have energy, resourcefulness, and perhaps musical ability). Lillian C has an original and booming business which started as a dog-walking service. It grew from that into one which included doing her customers' marketing, returning books to the library, taking shoes to be resoled, bringing children home from school. You might try selling cosmetics or books from door to door or shop to shop.

Or consider a beauty service—either your own or a booth in someone else's—where you have your own customers, hours, supply your own materials. You must have a license, be on your feet a lot; the crowded times are late afternoon and pre-weekend.

Ellen B was an art teacher with debts to pay. Her Monday-to-Friday job meant that any other must be free-lance. She searched near and far, and then found one on her doorstep. A block from school and from where she lived was a florist who wanted someone on Saturdays to make corsages and arrange floral decorations for weddings. Her artistic ability was a find for him, and the job a solution for her.

Free-lance possibilities are endless and individual. They depend on your talents, your initiative, and your neighborhood. No list could include opportunities for everyone, but perhaps these will serve as a spark for further ideas you might have and develop.

XII

GOVERNMENT

The government renders services to all people living in the United States. Some of these services are also rendered by private industry; some, like mail delivery, are unique to the government. The same jobs exist here as in business and the professions, are obtained in the same ways—through interviews, tests, training, experience. Titles may differ; salaries are in distinct categories. You can apply your interests and abilities, and advancement depends on you.

The Federal Government is the nation's largest employer; the city of New York is the second largest. One-tenth of the federal jobs are in Washington; others are throughout the country.

PERSONAL AND EDUCATIONAL QUALIFICATIONS. The Civil Service Commission, the central recruiting agency, judges qualifications in one of three ways: through examinations that measure aptitude, achievement, and other skills; through ratings based on experience and training; through sample evidence like drawings. Examinations are given only when there are openings, and government agencies select applicants from lists of successful candidates. Remember again, in reading about the jobs, that all are not available all the time.

Government jobs are open to U.S. citizens, although a few

positions go to non-citizens; state and city jobs may call for legal residence. There are minimum age requirements, but at the upper limits some positions accept applicants up to 70, and some states prohibit age discrimination. Not more than one member of a family under the same roof may hold a civil service job. There is no discrimination against race, color, national origin, marital status, politics, or sex, although a few jobs are necessarily restricted by sex (fire inspector to men; nurse to women).

College graduates take the Federal Service Entrance Examination (FSEE) during their junior or senior year, or after graduation, to qualify for careers. The FSEE is given continuously. Scientists, and some other majors, take a special examination which is open only from time to time.

You learn about openings from civil service announcements in your placement office, the Post Office, Civil Service Commission, State Employment Services, government agencies themselves, and representatives that come to the campus.

For jobs with the Foreign Service, Central Intelligence Agency, and National Security Agency, you write directly to their Washington offices; the FSEE does not cover these.

WORKING CONDITIONS. The government gives equal pay for equal work. Beginning wages compare well with those of other employers, but in the higher brackets are less than in private industry. Salaries are expressed in terms of a scale called a General Schedule (GS), with 18 grades, each having an upper limit to the salaries within its range. GS-1 is the lowest level; new college graduates generally enter at the GS-5 level—at GS-7 if they have graduate degrees or experience. These entrance salaries are about $300 apart. Increases are automatic within a grade; promotion to the next grade depends on further examination.

You are not likely to lose your job in bad times. Vacations, sick leave, retirement benefits, working hours are good. But on the negative side: you can be dismissed if you do not pay your bills; you may not take part in election campaigns or speculate on the stock market; you may live with red tape, in the form of multiple copies and involved regulations.

CAREERS IN THE GOVERNMENT. Since specific job descriptions in the professional and business fields are given elsewhere in this book, the following outline merely touches on *some* of the ways or places these jobs occur in government.

BUSINESS

You may enter any branch of the government as a *clerk, stenographer, typist, telephone operator,* or other office assistant, and learn from there.

AUTOMATION. Government agencies are conducting research programs on a wide range of subjects, through the use of electronic computing machines. The National Advisory Committee on Aeronautics, for example, studies basic mathematical theory for flight research.

BOOKKEEPING AND ACCOUNTING. The General Accounting Office reviews the financial transactions of the government and advises Congress on budgets; the Internal Revenue Service audits income tax returns, assists taxpayers, and examines their records in case of disagreement.

FINANCE. The Small Business Administration authorizes loans for expansion, capital equipment, or rehabilitation after flood damage, and analyzes and evaluates credit risks related to these loans. The Federal Housing Administration insures lending institutions against loss on loans on residential property. The Securities and Exchange Commission supervises the registration of stocks and bonds, suppresses fraudulent practices in the sale of securities, regulates stock exchanges, investment companies, and advisors.

INSURANCE. The Railroad Retirement Board administers an insurance system under which benefits are paid to aged or disabled railroad workers, wives, survivors. The Veterans' Administration helps war veterans and their beneficiaries.

The Department of Health, Education, and Welfare gives aid to crippled children, the blind, the aged. The Social Security Administration, an insurance agency, collects premiums in the form of taxes on wages, makes payments after retirements; *claims examiners* in state agencies interview applicants for unemployment insurance and determine the benefits they are entitled to.

INTERIOR DESIGN. *Decorators* are concerned with designing interiors, planning and selecting color schemes, furniture, upholstery, making estimates of costs and materials for the Smithsonian Institution and other agencies and museum collections.

MARKET RESEARCH. The Department of Commerce analyzes and interprets data concerning the economy of the country, progress of business, foreign and domestic trade, the transportation system. The Department of Agriculture acquires and distributes information for conservation of natural resources, stabilization of farm prices, and investigates new scientific methods.

PERSONNEL. All government agencies have personnel workers to recruit and counsel employees, do research, classify jobs, study salaries and wages. The Department of Labor assists job hunters and employers, maintains the State Employment Services in all states (free to applicants and employers), administers the Unemployment Insurance system, enforces laws concerning child labor, wages and hours, health, safety, workmen's compensation. The Women's Bureau issues many detailed publications on jobs, advice to specific groups like part-time or mature workers, and employment trends. Interviewers in local offices encourage applicants to read the *Civil Service Leader,* a newsstand publication listing and describing government jobs.

PUBLIC RELATIONS. *Writers* and *editors,* in practically all government agencies, issue materials for the press, radio, television, and put out periodicals and pamphlets in order to inform American citizens about government programs. *Information specialists* convert technical pieces into lay language for the public in order to increase understanding of government welfare programs. They write press releases, speeches for members of the cabinet, edit manuscripts to conform to government printing style, and plan exhibits.

Another kind of public relations effort is represented by bilingual port receptionists, at New York International Airport, working for the Department of Commerce. They meet foreign visitors to ease their way into this country, help them make out immigration forms, get their luggage, go through customs, find those who are meeting them, make train connections.

PUBLISHING.   The government, through countless publications, presents a picture of the United States to citizens. The Government Printing Office puts out inexpensive pamphlets on innumerable subjects to educate and help businessmen, farmers, hobbyists, home-owners, nurses, parents, teachers, and many others. (Typical variety of subjects: *Bibliography of North American Geology, Education Directory,* National Park System descriptive folders, *Public Papers of the Presidents of the United States, Tax Guide for Small Business*).

Printing officers give technical assistance in procuring, storing, and distributing materials, establishing production schedules, estimating costs, advising on methods of reproduction and selection of paper and binding.

The National Archives and Records Service is concerned with analyzing and evaluating government records in order to decide if they are worth preserving; cataloguing and classifying those which are; showing researchers how to use them.

RADIO.   The Federal Communications Commission regulates the activities of communication by wire and radio. It considers questions like these: What wave band should be assigned to international television? Ought programs be confined to news? The FCC sponsors studies of the impact of television on children.

The United States Information Agency, by radio, television, and the written word, prepares and sends world-wide messages of facts about America. The International Broadcasting Service (formerly Voice of America) sends messages to foreign countries in 38 languages. The International Motion Picture Service films and distributes motion pictures abroad.

REAL ESTATE. The Housing and Home Finance Agency affects entire urban communities by planning individual houses, building schools, setting up sewage systems. The Urban Renewal Administration works to clear and redevelop slum areas, prevent slums, and analyze mortgages.

PROFESSIONS

Archaeologists collect, classify, and preserve materials and prepare reports, for the Department of the Interior and the Smithsonian Institution.

Architects design and plan almost every type of structure.

Astronomers compute positions of the stars and planets, and plot the orbits of comets and asteroids, in order to prepare tables for air and sea navigators, at the Naval Observatory.

Bacteriologists, in the Department of Health, Education, and Welfare, specialize in medical, soil, or food bacteriology, vaccines, disinfectants, antibiotics for the prevention of disease.

Biologists conduct research applied to health, agriculture, and other sciences.

Cartographers measure and interpret data to determine the position, elevation, shape of topographic features, and the physical characteristics of bodies of water, for the Army Map Service, Geological Survey, Coast and Geodetic Survey.

Chemists conduct tests to learn the content and wholesomeness of food, see that it meets government requirements, study spoilage and ways of combatting it.

Curators prepare, classify, and maintain museum collections, supervise exhibits, lecture, answer questions that come in by mail.

Dental Hygienists assist dentists and dental surgeons in hospitals and on Indian reservations, for the Public Health Service and Veterans' Administration.

Dieticians in hospitals and outpatient clinics plan and supervise the preparation and serving of therapeutic diets, take care of equipment and storage, for the Veterans' Administration and the Department of Health, Education, and Welfare.

Docents take care of exhibits and do research on special music collections in the Smithsonian and other museums.

Entomologists classify the anatomy, physical habits, and responses of insects, and collect data on those injurious to man and animals, for the Department of Agriculture. (A marine biologist, editor-in-chief of the Fish and Wildlife Service, is author of two best-sellers about the sea and one on the dangers of pesticides.)

Geologists in the Atomic Energy Commission study mining districts.

Geophysicists investigate radioactive properties of the earth, for the Departments of Commerce, Navy, and Interior.

Home Economists oversee menus for military personnel, and do research for homemakers on scientific and safe canning methods; these are at the Department of Agriculture.

Illustrators make drawings of general and scientific subjects for publications, exhibits, identification.

Legal Aides examine documents, contracts, and claims filed by and against the government. Typical problem: does a man own the air space above his house, and if so, how much? when is a missile or satellite trespassing?

Librarians select, catalogue, classify publications in libraries serving government personnel and in most federal agencies. The Library of Congress issues copyrights for literary and artistic work published in this country. Books, pamphlets, magazines, music may qualify for copyright if they are properly reproduced and if two copies of the work are sent to the Library with the four-dollar fee.

Medical Record Librarians, in city hospitals, supervise and train personnel and see that records are complete and conform to regulations.

Nurses in hospitals minister to patients; in emergency rooms they take care of minor injuries and illnesses; under the Public Health Service they go to houses, schools, clinics to nurse the sick and promote good health.

Physicists measure time, mass, length, and structure of the atom, properties of materials, develop rockets, communications systems, and weapons for the defense agencies. Plans for landing a manned rocket on the moon were drawn up and tested by the National Aeronautics and Space Administration.

Physiologists study the adaptability of man to different climates and altitudes, and his reaction to acceleration and fatigue, for the Public Health Service and the Departments of the Army, Navy, and Air Force.

Psychologists give and interpret tests of intelligence, personality, interests, aptitudes; assist in the diagnosis of mental disturbances; study the characteristics of fatigue, learning, perception, for the Departments of the Air Force, Army, Navy, and Health, Education, and Welfare, and the Veterans' Administration.

Recreation Leaders supervise programs in hospitals and on military posts providing music, dances, theatre, and sports, and teach arts and crafts.

Social Workers help people develop their capabilities and solve their problems, for the Departments of Justice, Interior, Defense, and Health, Education, and Welfare, as well as the Veterans' Administration.

Teachers conduct elementary school classes on Indian reservations, and do rehabilitation work for the Departments of the Army and Navy and the Veterans' Administration; and under state agencies, instruct children of all ages, supervise teaching programs, work with social agencies on drop-outs.

For Further Information about Jobs or Training

American Society for Public Administration, 6042 Kimball Avenue, Chicago 37, Illinois

Public Personnel Administration, 1313 East 60th Street, Chicago 37, Illinois

XIII

INSURANCE

Insurance is one of the most far-reaching businesses in this country and it depends on safety in numbers. Basically, life insurance provides guaranteed funds whenever a policyholder dies (protection for wives, children, parents, brothers), but its function is not limited to paying *others* when something happens to *you*. Through insurance you can pay for an education (endowments is one way), prepare for your retirement (through annuities), be reimbursed for money stolen from you (fidelity bonding) or for business lost because your factory was not completed on schedule (surety bonding), replace a house burned down or swept away in a windstorm (fire and extended coverage), provide income for yourself after injury (liability).

When you buy accident insurance for your sailboat, the company agrees to pay you a sum of money if the boat is damaged. Like the coin tosser who knows what the chances are that heads will come up, the company knows what the probabilities are that your boat will run into trouble. The number of others in its class, skippered by sailors of your experience, navigated in similar waters, are some of the influences that provide a basis for the company's reasoning. The company charges you a rate (premium) that, added to premiums paid by other sailboat-owners, will enable it to pay you in case of accident and still stay in business. Each boat-owner then, by paying a small amount, can be sure of being covered in case of mishap because the risk is shared. Alone, his bill for the accident would be too high for him to manage.

From the jobholder's point of view, insurance could be described as majoring in people and minoring in numbers, or vice versa. Once upon a time there were three seniors. One of them was interested in working with people; one wanted a career in mathematics; one wanted to write. Basically, how-ever, all of them were at home with numbers; all got along with people. When they graduated they all found just what they wanted—in the same insurance company.

FOR THOSE MAJORING IN PEOPLE.   Agnes B is satisfying her interest in people through a job in the personnel department of a home office. She entered as an *underwriting trainee,* but after a few months found she did not enjoy the work. Since she liked the company and was doing well, she was transferred to the personnel office when an opening arose. After learning its function through clerical work on employee records, she was promoted to *interviewer;* as such she screened applicants for beginning jobs, and later was given the responsibility of referring them to suitable departments. Today she is *person-nel associate.* Her job includes visiting colleges to talk to seniors, calling employment agencies to describe job open-ings, and teaching misinformed applicants what the insurance field actually is. She frequently hands out copies of materials outlining job specifications, and suggests that applicants study the *Dictionary of Occupational Titles* for an understanding of particular duties.

Insurance entails being familiar with the changing eco-nomic and social needs of families, analyzing which of these can be met by insurance, deciding what policies could best meet the needs, making the policies available to the public through an agency's sales force, providing continuing service after the sale, and paying beneficiaries—plus the clerical and arithmetical operations involved in running the home office to carry these out.

Those who want to work with people, be outdoors a lot, free of desks, set their own hours, may be *life insurance under-writers (agents, saleswomen)*. They sell insurance but also do much more. Usually they have a contract with one company (a life insurance or a life and casualty insurance company) and work in one of its agencies or branch offices; they are on commission. Agents are called *brokers* when they represent several companies which provide different kinds of insurance. *Branch managers* are home-office employees, on the payroll. Advanced degrees are not required of agents; beginners are eligible for a trainee job, but should have had experience in some kind of job or in coping with living.

Agents work in cities, towns, rural areas, away from the home office.

Sarah H learned the business as a secretary to her husband in La Jolla. When they were married both were in their thirties; he was a life insurance agent. Because of a shortage of secretaries she offered to tide him over. She had imagination, a love of research, quick mind, friendly manner.

The first thing he asked her to do was make up a list of prospects. She read the newspapers, noted the names of new-comers in town, went through the telephone book, asked friends for suggestions, talked to members of her bridge club, then made appointments for her husband to see some of these.

In his initial visit, he got information about each person's needs, goals, finances, and the insurance already carried. On a second visit he presented a plan for approval with suggested policies to carry it out over the years (policies are contracts that have been worked out in advance). The agent made his suggestions according to his knowledge of the client's needs and budget. He used a rate book of tables which lists costs, time factors, and dividends of each policy—to select the most appropriate. When the client decided which policy to purchase, the agent helped him make out the application, scheduled the medical examination, saw that the policy was drawn up and put through. But his contact did not end there. He kept in touch with (serviced) each account, arranged for policy renewals in the case of casualty insurance, made adjustments necessitated by a change of address, a remarriage, change of job.

Mrs. H had a good deal to do with this. She learned the vocabulary, procedures, requirements as she collected filled-in applications. On casualty insurance she sent notices and bills to those whose annual payments were due; on life insurance she collected the carbon copies of premium notices and listed them for her husband's follow-up if necessary. She drafted letters for clients who wanted to arrange to have a newly adopted son made a beneficiary, or to ask if moving to another state would affect their policy, to borrow cash for an operation, or make a claim because of a fall on a neighbor's uneven pavement. Her husband would explain the details of these letters to clients, who would sign and send them to the home office for action.

After a year, Mrs. H resigned, but before she left, the company offered her a job as an agent if she took the examination for licensing. She put that in the back of her mind for a future day. The offer was made because people liked and trusted her, she knew how to plan time, was willing to study and work at a desk as well as at more active duties.

Claims adjusters, who investigate requests for payments in casualty insurance, also deal predominantly with people. After an automobile accident, for instance, they collect evidence, talk to the claimant, his doctor, the company doctor, witnesses, lawyers. They note discrepancies (a bystander reports that the car had been speeding; the driver denies it), iron out differences. Or they study requests for hospital or disability payments, compare the various reports, work out the best alternative, arrange for benefits to be paid. Claims adjusters must understand legal and medical terms, have good judgment, tact, courtesy, and integrity.

FOR THOSE WHO LIKE NUMBERS. Work that goes on at the office is concerned with figures. After Mr. H's fact-finding interview he may calculate how much insurance it will take for a wealthy man to provide the cash and income he wants his family to have for expenses while his capital is tied up during the settlement of his estate; how a father can provide for larger income during his children's growing years, and less after that; how much income an annuity would provide a woman wanting to invest a certain sum. He thus acts as a financial advisor, making recommendations on the basis of his knowledge of social security, estate matters, and the taxes affecting the client's life insurance.

When the home office gets the application from him, *underwriters* (not to be confused with life insurance underwriters who sell) go over it with pencil, paper, mathematical know-how. (Historically, underwrite means to write one's name under as being accountable for loss or damage.) The home office underwriters' job is to decide if an applicant would be a good risk and whether or not to insure him. They consider his age, marital status, financial standing, position in the community, occupation (a riveter's premium will be higher than a gardener's), health, hobbies, medical history (tendency to some diseases is inherited), the results of his physical examination. They decide if the amount of insurance asked for is in line with his income and property. They may find that he is a standard risk (and give him the lowest rate), or a substandard risk (in which case he must pay a higher rate).

The underwriter needs basic arithmetical ability, consistent judgment, a thorough knowledge of insurance, ability to read medical reports, familiarity with all sorts of occupations, understanding of finances, and skill at seeing between the lines (an unexplained gap in jobs may point to temporary unemployment, illness, a misdemeanor—which may or may not have significance).

The premium rates that the underwriter uses (and which form the contents of the agents' rate books) have been calculated by *actuaries*. They work with pads, actuarial manuals, machines, and formulas like $C_x = v^{x+1} d_x$; they know how many men of 30 are apt to live how many years. They study statistical tables (some of which they worked out themselves), take into account the cost of running the business and the expected interest on the company's legal reserve funds (the amounts the law requires it to keep on hand). These funds are invested and make possible loans to policyholders, useful in times of depression or emergencies.

Actuaries also do research to develop new forms of insurance. (Radiation hazard brought a different approach.) They study costs, estimate dividends to policyholders, accumulate a body of medical information and longevity data.

Some actuaries go on to become heads of other departments or company officers. Still others branch out and serve as consultants to banks, labor unions, business firms, the government.

Most actuaries start as trainees after college with a major in mathematics. Beginners who have not gone to college work as clerks and do the arithmetic in the separate steps.

Group insurance, taken out by employers for their employees, includes workmen's compensation (for injury or death of a person while on the job); disability insurance (which reimburses workers for a certain amount of wages not paid during prolonged illness or accident); pension systems (which pay employees on retirement); group life, health, and accident insurance.

The same general steps are followed as with individual policies, with some others added. In the group department *calculators* work out sample plans for prospective buyers to consider, record names, ages, retirement dates, and names of beneficiaries, estimate premiums (payroll is one of the ingredients), review policies regularly to determine changes in their cost to the employer. They work with figures, machines, state insurance laws.

A PLACE FOR WRITERS.   Everyone in the insurance business must be able to write clearly. Some in group insurance, for instance, put technical material into lay terms for promotional booklets which describe plans to the employees. Others answer policyholders' questions by translating technical terms into everyday language. A person's fire insurance is no longer in effect because he has moved to a house beyond reach of the fire department; a *correspondent* writes to explain the increased premium cost. Some are in constant touch with claimants, to describe the different ways payments may be made, the rights of policyholders to assign ownership, make loans, change methods of payment.

And, on the other hand, *policy form drafters* with a logical mind, good English, and skill reverse the process and put information into legal language.

Other work with the written word occurs at various stages. One job is the designing and printing of policies and group insurance forms that the company has decided to offer (certificate analysis). It involves a study of existing forms, an understanding of insurance terms and printing processes, preparing the make-up for the printer, and okaying the finished product.

OTHER JOB POSSIBILITIES.   Because so many kinds of information are needed in the operation of insurance, specialists in practically every field find opportunities here: *doctors* examine prospective individual policyholders (no examination is required for group insurance); *nurses* and *medical technicians* assist doctors and patients, or analyze results; *tax* and *investment experts* advise on the use of the company's income; *lawyers* assist in settling claims; *copywriters* produce mailing pieces, premium enclosures, or advertisements showing the uses of insurance; *public relations writers* turn out news stories, magazine articles, speeches; *editors* run company house organs; *educational directors* supervise training programs; *engineers* examine industrial plants and estimate damages to them; *architects* judge conditions of new buildings; *programmers* set up machines to solve problems, prepare premium notices, calculate benefits, write checks; *auditors* check agency and branch-office accounts.

OPPORTUNITIES FOR WOMEN. Life and casualty insurance are good areas; but fire insurance is not a business for women because climbing fire escapes, inspecting unfinished buildings, testing fire equipment, examining water damage are part of the job. Office jobs have normal hours; agents may have to suit their hours to those of the client. Women who want to work only part time find openings in coding and key punch operating at home offices. Returners who have the ability can go on to more advanced work.

Half a million people work in the life insurance field, only about one-third of whom are women and most of these do office work. Only a small proportion are life insurance underwriters (agents), not because there is prejudice against them (which there is and isn't), but because many women do not like to sell. They forget that all of us are selling every day: college professors are salesmen when they lecture; trial lawyers, when in court; and you are, when you look and act your best in a job interview or at a party. A variety of opportunities abound, for in one city you can find the cosmopolitanism of a big home office, or the individuality of an agent's office, and therefore choose the size and atmosphere you want.

Most insurance workers are in the home offices in Connecticut, Texas, Massachusetts, California, but many are employed in agencies, brokerage firms, and other sales offices in cities and towns everywhere.

College graduates start as *trainees,* others in various beginning jobs. Graduate degrees are not needed except for the professional; you learn as you work, and later take the additional courses you need. Beginning salaries are better than in many fields.

New developments make this field an expanding one. The population growth means more people to want insurance; medical discoveries are turning substandard risks into standard ones; state laws are making more insurance mandatory (workmen's compensation and disability insurance used to be voluntary; automobile insurance is now required in some parts of the country); new risks such as insecticides create new types of insurance.

For Further Information about Jobs or Training

Health Insurance Institute, 488 Madison Avenue, New York 22, New York

Institute of Life Insurance, Women's Division, 488 Madison Avenue, New York 22, New York

Insurance Information Institute, 110 William Street, New York 38, New York

Life Office Management Association, 110 East 42nd Street, New York 17, New York

National Association of Life Underwriters, 11 West 42nd Street, New York 18, New York

Society of Actuaries, 208 South LaSalle Street, Chicago 4, Illinois

XIV

INTERIOR DESIGN

Most women are decorators at heart, whether they choose the venetian blinds for their house, rearrange their office furniture, or straighten other people's pictures. But decorating for fun or for work are poles apart. When you express a wish to turn the avocation into a vocation, remember you must be trained ahead of time for this profession; you may not learn on the job. Besides, after you master certain techniques and acquire certain knowledge, you then reckon with something not present in your avocation—the customer who, like the camel, has *her* plans.

Interior design—the term which has replaced decorating to show how much the field encompasses, although those in it are often called decorators still—is for gregarious artists who are skillful with arithmetic and mechanics. Professional standing calls for a college degree and experience. Age is a premium; the young do not inspire the same confidence.

NO CUTTING CORNERS ON EDUCATION. You cannot take courses just in modern design because that is your forte: you may have to decorate a Southampton house, Cape Cod cottage, Hawaiian night club (no stripes of complementary colors, they make you dizzy), an Illinois factory, Hollywood theatre, or a one-room apartment (light walls will make it seem larger). You study the history of architecture and of furniture, learn to build a room around an heirloom you may dislike. You must know woods: which ones splinter, which are hard, which good for moldings. You must see things as a whole; it is not enough to be able to choose draperies, upholster chairs. You don't just match or contrast colors, you *use* them: ceilings look lower if they are dark, higher if painted the same as the walls; black in direct light is lighter than white in shadow. You know fabrics, floor coverings, sizes (an average chair is 1'6" from the floor, doorways are at least three feet wide); heights (a bookcase may be seven feet high, but not a kitchen cabinet).

WHEN YOU REACH THE TOP AND BECOME A DESIGNER. You must be able to lay out an entire house, abiding by the dimensions given; visualize from the floor plan; dream up alternatives when the architect says you have put the hi-fi equipment where the fireplace must be, or a stove at the head of the basement stairs. Your sense of design is applied not only to the familiar mantelpiece balance, influenced by the fulcrum principle, but to the total effect: a room seen through another and across the hall; the picture beside a window overlooking the swimming pool.

You need tact, persuasion, conviction, the right amount of willingness to give in to clients. You must talk their language, make watercolors to convey what you have in mind. You work with pencil, pen, T square, compass, mechanical drawing instruments, airbrush, a three-sided ruler that converts feet directly into scales in inches. You read blueprints, know how to sketch quickly but accurately (notice how draperies fall into triangles); you construct cardboard models of furniture to show different arrangements, convert floor plans into perspective paintings.

You estimate cost, know prices, stay within budgets, pare down without compromising. When the plans are approved,

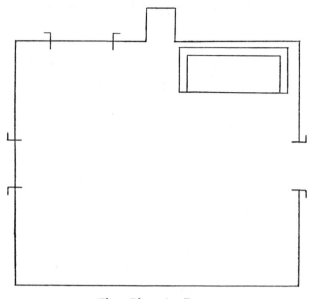

Floor Plan of a Room

you order materials, have curtains made up, buy paintings, oversee carpet laying, arrange tables and sofas.

You must like the work *and* those around you. Clarissa N, just out of college, wanted to have a career in decorating. After pounding New York pavements for several weeks she landed a secretarial job with a decorator. But in a month she gave it up saying that she wanted to be creative but not around creative people.

You might start as *apprentice* to a decorator, taking measurements for materials to be ordered, shopping for textiles, getting samples, doing office work. In an antique shop you learn pieces and periods, ways of redoing tapestries or broken inlays. *Selling* in department stores will give you a line on customers, teach you how to complete sales. At wallpaper houses you might *render designs*. (Can you do repeats, showing how a pattern will look all over, not just in one spot?)

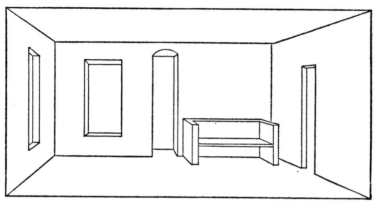

Three-Dimensional Drawing Made from Floor Plan of a Room

You learn that any color looks darker on a wall than in a small sample.

Olivia M got a very unusual job for a girl and one which made good use of her talents. She specialized in dramatics in college and learned stage production. She was artistic and mechanical. Through a professor she got a job right after graduation with a theatrical service which supplies equipment for amateur and professional groups. At first she was a runner, searching for scenery, picking up costumes, delivering props. Then she worked in the office taking orders for backdrops, masks, lighting, and helped producers select what they needed. She had a chance to do ordering and answer questions about where to get costumes for a certain period, furniture typical of a given country, or lighting for a particular effect. Next she worked with theatre architects, pointing out acoustical problems, advising on number of seats, shape of the stage, spotlight angles. Her practical experience made very meaningful the formal training she decided to take to become professional.

IF YOU SET UP YOUR OWN SHOP.   You must have a business head. You might specialize in an area familiar to you. You know the sequence that determines the arrangement of kitchen equipment, will see that the sink is not flush with the floor but has room for toes. You will advise a restaurant to include low tables and chairs for children (very successful at one on a busy highway in Fort Wayne, which flatters tired children and keeps them quiet); you will place bedroom light fixtures at the right angle for applying make-up.

JOB OPPORTUNITIES. Interior design, often called a luxury business, is actually aimed at all income groups, and is practiced in large cities and their suburbs. *Decorators,* and here that term is correct, are employed by department stores and furniture shops to advise customers and decorate the shop and windows; some work for hotels, architects, manufacturers, magazines that feature articles on home furnishings, and office planners, who may design a round room for meetings or special brokerage desks with built-in telephones.

The field is becoming increasingly complex: you are expected to be familiar with landscape architecture, installation of air conditioning, industrial space planning, engineering problems. Hours are long and irregular because they often must fit those of the client. A liability is the client who takes your time, does not engage you, or changes her mind. Interior design is not easy to get into or to count on when you do.

WHEN YOU JOB HUNT. Have a portfolio of your paintings, drawings, photographs. Include designs of rooms or houses you have sketched. If you have no such demonstrations to show, then collect samples of your taste—layouts you like, pictures of rooms you find pleasing, shapes or colors you would put together. Show *how* you work and think.

For Further Information about Jobs or Training

American Institute of Interior Designers, 673 Fifth Avenue, New York 22, New York

National Society of Interior Designers, Inc., 157 West 57th Street, New York 19, New York

XV

MARKET RESEARCH

When you're called to the telephone and asked what TV program you're watching, or when your doorbell is rung by someone who wants to know if you use pressed or loose face powder, you have become a part of market research. Sometimes you have if you just take a box of cereal off the supermarket shelf.

WHAT IS MARKET RESEARCH? It is a method of trying to increase sales by finding out how people react to an advertisement, product, or corporation. Strictly speaking the term applies to just that and nothing more. But actually, because the same techniques are used, it also refers to:

Consumer Research (the term often used interchangeably with market research). To learn how customers react to a new product or design, how well the product is selling (before sales figures can be obtained), who is buying the product (men, women, young, old, and at what economic levels).

Product Testing. A laboratory check on the quality of a product, or a study of the consumer's attitude toward it.

Sales Testing. Finding out how much is sold by certain stores, how well a selected market responds to a specific advertising campaign; or measuring nationwide sales levels.

Dealer Testing. The subject interviewed is the retailer or middleman rather than the consumer.

Media Testing. Is it better to advertise in a magazine or on a road sign?

Copy Testing. Finding out the best way to use the media selected.

A closely related field is *public opinion research,* which covers a wide range of subjects of social concern such as foreign trade, social security, attitudes toward education; it also includes political polling. Another major type of research is *public relations research,* the effort to discover the attitudes of various segments of the public toward organizations, corporations, other groups, or individuals.

The newest addition to this fast-growing field is *motivation research: why* people prefer certain products, rather than *which* products they prefer. Information is elicited through a conversational method, not a predetermined set of questions. Possible finding: a salad dressing is unpopular because of its color.

The term, market research, then, covers the statistical process of determining how many people behave or think this way or that, deciding what the information means, and how to use it to advantage.

Suppose a manufacturer wants to know the best time to reach radio listeners who might buy his new folding tables. Do they do the breakfast dishes to a soap opera at ten o'clock in the morning or are they shopping then? Through questioning a number of people and treating the results with certain formulas, he will get his answer.

Market research has been criticized for not being scientific when findings were not in line with what actually happened later. But criticism should be directed at specific studies and the way they are treated, not at the basic method, which is as sound as the ability and integrity of those who apply it.

FOR THOSE WHO WANT JOBS DEALING WITH PEOPLE. Applicants can begin as *interviewers* who hand out or mail questionnaires or call people on the telephone, recording answers on the printed sheet. They may have to interview a given number of people a day, drive all over the state, or work for ten straight days including weekends. Or they may work conveniently on their own time, in their own neighborhood. They will meet many reactions: be insulted by those who think the questions impertinent, be offered coffee by garrulous women, have doors slammed in their faces. They must take it all. Incomplete questionnaires are not counted, and tact is often needed to persuade reluctant housewives to answer the last few questions.

The *supervisor of the interviewing department* does the hiring and the training. She may travel to various parts of the country to get local people to do the work; she may hire those in her own area; or she may send the work to her list of housewives across the nation. Mrs. V, a Florida housewife with two small children, tries out new refrigerators for the manufacturer and reports her criticism. (One such report: 12 compartments for eggs are not enough, because when a woman goes to market for a dozen eggs, she usually has one or two left in the icebox.)

When questionnaires are completed, the supervisor makes a spot check by telephoning or reinterviewing about 10 per cent of those questioned to be sure they were really approached and that a tired interviewer did not make up the answers herself!

The questionnaire is originally set up by a *statistician* who first decides who is to be studied. Since it is impossible to interview all potential buyers, the sampling technique must be used: that is, the selection of a sample having the same characteristics, and in the same proportion, as the total population. Researchers word the questions, an art in itself since they must frame them so as not to influence the answers: "Do you eat one slice of toast for breakfast, or two?" will reveal more toast eaters than "What do you eat for breakfast?"

FOR THOSE WHO WANT TO DEAL WITH FIGURES. When the questionnaires have been completed and spot-checked, they are ready for the *coders* and *tabulators,* who may be beginners, or seasoned employees working on complex problems. Coders assign a number or letter to each part of every answer to facilitate adding them up. Yes-and-no questions can be coded ahead of time (pre-coded), but those which are answered by sentences cannot be coded until all responses are in and the variety known. Tabulators then do the addition by machine.

These figures are put into percentages which *statistical typists* set up in tables for study and explanation; the accuracy of the raw data and of the percentages is checked, and conclusions drawn about what is significant. (If more boots were sold in Milwaukee than in Chicago, does that mean a better market there or merely more snow?)

Next this technical information is translated into terms that will be meaningful to others. A *chartist* helps by drawing graphs, diagrams, and other pictorial devices to accompany and clarify the written account. This comprises the finished report which goes to the *research director* for discussion with the client.

The whole analytic process is done by *senior researchers* and *analysts,* assisted by *junior researchers.* Holders of these positions need to understand statistical formulas and their uses, sometimes devise formulas, work with tables and adding machines, know the normal distribution curve, analysis of variants, probabilities.

IF YOU LIKE RESEARCH BUT NOT NUMBERS. There are jobs for *librarians* who supply information on what has already been done on the subject. They must know card catalogues, reference books and how to use them, indexes, and outside sources. A junior researcher comes in again to study these findings to see if they will help the present study or indicate that it needn't be made.

Editors correct inconsistent spellings, note omissions, clarify illegible handwriting of completed questionnaires, and reject those that can't be used.

PERSONAL QUALIFICATIONS FOR MARKET RESEARCH. You should be wrapped up in figures, feel with them, understand what they mean and don't mean, and see everything through mathematical eyes. You should have a nagging curiosity that keeps you always thirsting for more information or looking for a new angle on what you have. You should be interested in people, able to get along with them (and that means not just the unpredictable public but the doubting Thomas who may be your client), be able to express yourself clearly on paper. But the mathematical instinct is paramount, and you can't get along without it in the long run.

Theresa L majored in economics in college and became a field interviewer for a manufacturing company after graduation. She interviewed housewives, businessmen, and children in 50 cities, and then became a field supervisor, doing the hiring and training of interviewers throughout the country. After three years she wanted to stop traveling, and so she joined an oil company as assistant analyst, forecasting production and marketing. Family circumstances required her to go east, and she got a job in an advertising agency as assistant field director, becoming field director a year later. Now she is in charge of an office staff of seven, field staff of 200, and 1,500 interviewers. She estimates costs of surveys, establishes probability samples, and supervises copy tests, depth interviews, telephone surveys, store audits, and readership studies.

Although it's still a man's world at the top, women do have their own market research firms. Besides, it is a field that lends itself to the particular restrictions women often have to put on a job: there are lots of part-time and temporary jobs, and also home work because the studies may be short, one-shot assignments.

One woman who had five years of experience in a market

research firm set up her own office when she married. Operating from her apartment, taking on spot assignments from businesses, she has been able to keep her office going while bringing up her children.

If the temporary or part-time aspect interests you rather than the career possibilities, remember that interviewing appeals to those who want to be on the go, enjoy an outdoor job, and truly like all kinds of people. Tabulating is for those who are accurate, unafraid of figures, and who prefer paper work and an office job.

EDUCATION AND TRAINING REQUIREMENTS.   A high school education will get you into interviewing, coding, and tabulating. College graduates may be *called* trainees but will start with the same basic jobs. Chartists need some experience with art or mechanical drawing. A college education is needed for the other jobs, preferably a degree with a major in economics, English, psychology, sociology, or statistics, or else an equivalent amount of experience plus courses in statistics. But college, with *any* major, will get you on your way, and later you can add the specific courses plus the Ph.D. which is helpful for the advanced jobs. One senior had a job interviewing classmates for a study conducted by a radio network. The reports she turned in were so clear and accurate that she received a special bonus; and when she graduated she landed an interviewing job immediately even though there was a recession and jobs were scarce.

WHERE OPENINGS ARE.   The jobs occur in advertising agencies, market research firms, public opinion offices, sociological and political research organizations, hospitals, business and industrial firms, manufacturing, retail stores, scientific firms, trade and professional organizations, management engineering, and the government. New York and Chicago have the largest number of market researchers, but there are opportunities in other cities also.

ABOUT THE PAY.   Starting salaries compare well with those

in other fields. Housewives who do product-testing at home get the use of the ever-latest model and perhaps a pittance. Part-time interviewers are on an hourly basis, and earn somewhat less than part-time secretaries; they receive carfare for local travel, and room and board if overnight is involved; those trained to do specialized depth interviewing command a great deal more. The future is as good as in any business field.

USE MARKET RESEARCH METHODS TO GET YOURSELF A JOB. If you decide that market research is for you, apply it to your job hunt. Learn its vocabulary. Find out where research is being done on subjects that are connected with women—clothes, kitchen equipment, household utensils. After all, you are more likely to be hired for a study of children's toys than of safety devices for trucks.

If you are married and still tied to the house, know what your limitations are about hours; find out which companies use people for home studies *before* you apply to them.

Show that you have an instinct for market research by pointing up your job hunt through a research of your own market.

For Further Information about Jobs or Training

American Marketing Association, 27 East Monroe Street, Chicago 3, Illinois

American Association for Public Opinion Research, 570 Lexington Avenue, New York 17, New York

XVI

PERSONNEL—PLACEMENT—EXECUTIVE RECRUITING

PERSONNEL

Personnel work is concerned with the employees in an organization as opposed to its products, machinery, sales, or services. Its function is to see that the staff runs smoothly so that the business does.

Originally when companies were small, and even today if they are, this function was handled by the owner or manager. As business grew in size and intricacy, and as theories of psychology and efficiency developed, this job became a separate skill, too much for the executive officer to take on, too specialized for others.

You must like all temperaments, ages, backgrounds, and intelligence if you go into personnel work, and there are no two ways about it. That does not mean you will meet people all day—in fact you may see few—but it does mean you must be really interested in them for the good of your company. You can use many of your talents. Chances are, though, that whatever route you follow you will have as much paper along the way as people. For personnel is not all people. Applicants for this work have said to interviewers, "I would love a job like yours where I talk to people all day." Talking is what shows, but even interviewers have much note-taking to do in recording their impressions and estimations of applicants, comments of others, what follow-up was indicated, what taken, the final outcome; answering letters of application, reviewing data sheets, checking, making recommendations.

Your tools are pencils, forms, files, résumés, telephone books, newspapers, salary and tax tables, payroll cards, trade journals that keep you up on new personnel procedures.

Whatever angle absorbs you eventually, the way in is usually office work. Typing is your skill, papers your material, details your concern. As a *clerk* you might put new employees on the payroll, note the date hired, results of physical examinations, wages, amounts of withholdings, job title, department. You keep these records up to date, note changes of address, marital status, exemptions. You record hours worked, vacations earned, sick leave due. You discuss pay checks with employees, answer questions about totals (smaller this month because they worked fewer hours, or because social security taxes rose), substitute for the receptionist during her lunch hour, answer the telephone.

With luck you might go in as a *receptionist-interviewer*. As such you see job applicants who drop in, turn away those obviously unqualified (translators applying to an office that does no international work), administer and score tests, telephone employment agencies to list job openings or notify them when they are filled. Your function is to sift.

Employment interviewer is one job ahead of you. You see applicants for all sorts of jobs, from clerk and elevator starter to biochemist or textile designer. You decide if applicants meet requirements and then refer them to the departments that need them. You keep a file of employment agencies, visit them from time to time, maintain a list of classified sections to advertise in, search out other sources of personnel. You post notices of openings which might interest the current staff. You will interview many who do not qualify because of training or experience (too little or too much), or personality characteristics (an impatient person applying for a job of inspecting watch parts), or education (an economics major without statistics wanting to do investment research). You will find yourself advising them about preparation, other employers, fields, methods of job hunting, and suggesting to them references like *Occupational Literature.*

Counseling is another job dealing directly with people. It may be a department in itself, or part of another. Its purpose is to show employees how to plan to get ahead, or to help them with personal troubles or those connected with their jobs. These may range from problems of finding a day nursery for a pre-school child to those of getting along with a fellow worker, or of planning how to ease financial adjustments after retirement. Counselors refer to directories of residence houses, hospitals, legal aids, social services, consult supervisors, staff assistants, outside advisors. A degree in psychology is sometimes expected.

OPPORTUNITIES TO TEACH occur in the training department. Eleanor J left the education field to go into business. She was hired by a factory and first given a course in its machines, taught to read blueprints, micrometers, engineering symbols. Then she was ready to train new employees, describe the company's history, policy, rules and privileges (holidays, vacations, rest periods), and direct the program that taught workers their jobs.

Safety administration is a part of personnel work and it is not easy. Women working with machine tools may have to be convinced to wear bandannas (to prevent their hair from getting caught), flat-heeled shoes, gloves (to protect them from coolants), goggles (to stop flying particles), and to remove their rings. They must be taught not to stand directly behind an o.d. grinder since the wheel may fly off, to put one foot behind the other when pulling a large wrench toward them, in case it slips. Some cautious people accept the instructions;

others buck them. It is your job to explain and enforce the regulations, oversee posters and folders printed for your campaign, talk to employees in groups and individually, enlist the help of the medical department.

If your company sends representatives to colleges to interview seniors for jobs after graduation, this recruiting may fall to you. You plan these trips, write to placement offices telling them your itinerary, describe the qualifications you are looking for, send brochures about your company and its jobs, ask for appointments on certain days. You may spend weeks on the road, going from college to college, seeing students who are interested in your company and their classmates who are not. You offer some of them jobs on the spot, invite others to visit your office during vacation, tell still others they are not cut out for this work. You meet students, faculty, vocational directors; keep records; take part in vocational conferences.

Other duties concerned directly with people include visiting employees in the hospital, helping workers find jobs after layoffs, organizing clambakes, badminton tournaments, 25th-anniversary award dinners, tuition refund plans.

OTHER APPROACHES. You might do personnel work in the capacity of *office manager,* assigning and overseeing the work of the secretaries, typists, and clerks; proofread, watch supplies, organize and set up files, hire and train. Your primary concern is running the office, but includes personnel duties.

Sometimes there is no actual personnel department, and the person in charge has other duties besides. Betty C interviews and hires for a publishing house, and is also secretary to an editor; Laura P takes care of employee benefits in a paper mill, and is editor of the house organ.

Usually you must have experience in or knowledge of the business of the company so as to understand and clarify its jobs. Store personnel interviewers who have gone through the training program realize the demands of a selling job and judge applicants' qualifications; those who have operated lathes and drill presses know if a worker is malingering when she says the oil is giving her a rash.

IF YOU HAVE A LEGAL TURN OF MIND, labor relations is a line to consider. There is prejudice against women in this area, the work is rough, hours are late, but if they can take it, their patience pays off. Good labor relations means good rapport between employer and employee. You listen to union representatives defend a worker who claims he was fired without cause; or you try to meet the unusual and difficult union request that a movie cashier live in the theatre's neighborhood. You work on contracts and try to coordinate the demands of union leaders with those of your management.

A legal or accounting bent is useful in wage and salary administration. Here you see that fair rates are paid for the jobs performed. You keep up with labor laws, fair employment practices, minimum wage requirements, and salaries paid by other employers. You observe workers on their jobs, see how much they turn out in a given time, show them short cuts, reduce wasted effort. Such time-and-motion studies are a touchy area, require tact. If a cutter sees you counting the number of coats he does per hour, he may try to work faster, yet may fear that if he does he will be expected to maintain that level consistently. You must allay suspicion but get facts.

FOR RESEARCHERS.   A statistical interest can take you into research. Starting as a *personnel assistant* you can work on studies related to job performance: causes of turnover, absenteeism, lateness; effect of air conditioning, soundproofing, comfortable chairs. One finding: greater output when lighting is stepped up, then greater again when it is reduced; *change* is the stimulus. You interview employees to learn their attitudes about present conditions or prospective changes (early opening and closing plus shorter lunch periods to avoid rush-hour traffic). You tabulate results of interviews, work up charts to give a graphic picture of results. This job usually calls for psychology majors who have studied statistics.

Research work of a different kind lies in job analysis and evaluation. This department studies each job, breaks down its duties, time required, training needed, degree of responsibility, and holds periodic discussions with employees to review their performance. It writes specifications (specs) for selecting applicants and placing them suitably, and it watches for changes in job functions (an office worker may have to learn new machines or make independent decisions which change the job, wages, and perhaps title).

Writers find opportunities in research studies, employee newsletters, instruction manuals, orientation pamphlets, booklets for job hunters giving information about the company, and in composing classified advertisements: no cinch since ads must be eye-catching to attract the competent yet worded to screen out those interested who don't measure up.

Top-level titles include: *director* or *manager of personnel* or of *industrial, labor,* and *employee relations.*

EDUCATIONAL AND PERSONAL REQUIREMENTS. You can go into this field from high school or, better, from college. Look for a job in a personnel department, or simply get in the company; if you have an aptitude for personnel work, you will be discovered. You don't have to specialize in any course though some employers prefer a major in personnel administration, but when you take additional study it might be in American history, business administration, economics, English, personnel management, psychology, sociology, statistics, vocational testing, writing—or for that matter, almost anything that interests you because it is bound to be useful.

You should read newspapers, keep up with labor disputes and their causes, like detail, understand motives, have a good memory, be persuasive, honest, able to keep confidences, say No to applicants, above all—listen.

Personnel work is particularly suited to women, but their

superiors are usually men. It makes fewer uses of part-time assistance than some other fields. Salaries are normal and can go high for specialists. It is, though, a business that reflects setbacks in the economy. Jobs occur in every field all over the country, the more highly organized departments being in large companies, big cities, major plants.

PLACEMENT

In personnel work you generally deal with people you know, since they are your fellow employees; in placement your acquaintance with each person is relatively brief.

Placement work is the process of finding people and jobs and putting them together. It is fast-moving, pressured, varied, detailed, highly competitive.

An agency may consist of one person, the *manager, owner,* or *licensee,* who does executive and clerical work; or it may have a large staff of *placement managers (interviewers), typists,* and a *receptionist.* Some specialize in certain fields (publishing, bookkeeping, non-profit); some in certain salaries (only the upper brackets).

If you start as a *receptionist,* you greet applicants, check to see whether they have an appointment (often preferred with the experienced), or, if not, find out whether anyone can interview them now. Usually the answer is yes: agencies try to squeeze in as many people as they can. You give them applications, see that they are completed and legible; introduce applicants to the interviewers; answer telephones, often three or more at once; hold calls, keep track of who is on which line, see that callers are not cut off or kept waiting too long; call newspapers to list jobs to be advertised, and describe jobs to applicants over the telephone. You convert yearly salaries into monthly or weekly rates—whichever form is familiar to the applicant; keep a register of placements: the date, employer, starting salary, references, amount of the fee, date of the job order and of the placement; write down simple job descriptions on form cards, check references, file applications (either alphabetically or by job request, with a kardex or a flag system).

By observation and direction you learn to become a skillful *interviewer,* to get much information in a short time: income depends on making placements; therefore the more people you see, the greater the chances of placements. The facts you need appear on the application; you must supply the sensitivity or dexterity to elicit the information between the lines. You must spot falsifications—a birth date out of line with a graduation date; recognize signs of emotional disturbance— not necessarily a detriment, as Mrs. B proved when she placed as laundress a woman with a hand-washing compulsion; draw out the taciturn and keep the loquacious on the track; cut interviews short when you have learned what you need, without letting the applicant feel shortchanged—experienced interviewers can learn much in a brief time. You tell some to come back after they have learned to type; refer others to jobs by arranging appointments for them or letting them make their own; explain the terms of the contract (their agreement to pay a fee and to keep your information confidential); outline job duties; criticize résumés.

Janet L had excellent preparation in physics, a subject not usually associated with placement work. After college she taught mathematics at an independent school, then went into Communications in the WAVES. When she returned to civilian life, she joined an employment agency. Her use of the scientific method in reserving judgment, examining facts, weighing evidence, enables her to size up applicants, gauge statements: a complaint about poor working conditions or inconsiderate employers may be valid or the hysteria of a disgruntled employee.

Seeing people is only part of the job. After talking to applicants the interviewer writes her comments, records jobs she referred them to, makes corresponding notations on the job order cards, is careful about dates.

You discuss with employers complex job orders for technical or experienced personnel, learn the exact speed of dictation required of a stenographer, the kind of person wanted, the future opportunities. You telephone or visit companies to solicit jobs; go through your files to find applicants who qualify; reach applicants by telephone, postcard, or telegram; or send résumés to companies who prefer to see these before the applicants.

You must keep up with changing jobs and titles, know the fields appearing on the horizon (television was new once), typical salaries for different subjects and amounts of experience; in short, you must know the employment market *today*.

There are frustrations. Some applicants refuse to fill out an application, forcing you to extract through lengthy conversation what you could learn at a glance; others accept through another source a job they said did not interest them. Employers complain you have sent them no one, when you actually referred several who never applied. Some employers change their minds as they go along, lean heavily on you to help them make decisions; others are hard to reach and then hire someone without reporting it.

There are also the satisfactions of placing people in jobs they like, and these can outweigh frustrations or low revenue: the retired social worker you place in a job that pays her enough to swell her pension and yet not jeopardize her social security; the girl who took your advice and learned shorthand and then got just what she wanted in television; the long unemployed psychologist whom you placed in a job that called for an economist; the understanding companion you found for the worried man with an invalid wife.

PERSONAL QUALIFICATIONS. Beginning jobs require that you get on with people; the office skills needed will vary but seldom include stenography. Some states require interviewers and owners to meet certain requirements of psychological training or personnel experience.

Agencies are licensed by their state, and laws govern their fees, record keeping, location, and the fields they cover: the same agency may not handle theatrical, domestic, teaching, and office jobs.

Starting your own agency is virtually only a matter of pump-priming. You establish an office, send out announcements and advertisements to reach the people you want, thereby cause a backlog of jobs and applicants, and you are on your way. Many women own and operate their own agencies, some even part time. Mrs. U has had an office for ten years. A believer in part-time jobs, she specializes in them and has made one for herself. She does all the work; her office is open only part of the day. She locks up when she leaves early or takes off for vacations with her husband and children; clients know her schedule and call her when she is back.

Beginners in office jobs earn salaries at the going rate; those who do placement work may receive a small salary, but usually get only commissions, from their own placements or from placements made by others in jobs they themselves brought in. Hours are long because the more you work, the more you make; many lunches are on the run or at your desk.

It is a field for those who have energy, physical and emotional strength, good humor; who like ringing telephones, constant traffic, sudden calms in seasonal dips.

EXECUTIVE RECRUITING

The management consultant firm specializing in executive recruiting is another form of personnel and placement work. Although few women are engaged in it, a discussion of this field would be incomplete without it.

Management consultants, as outside individuals or firms, have for years advised companies on problems of finance, cost accounting, marketing, production, or on how to get established in the first place. Executive recruitment, a new area of specialization, is the process of finding qualified executive personnel for business, industrial, or professional organizations.

These firms, which are to be found in large cities, are in touch with companies all over the country, work with employment agencies, keep up with top personnel, note news of executive changes, watch the progress of key men, know when one is ready to move up to the next stage of his career, when he is blocked in his own company. They round up résumés and recommendations, act as the representative of an anonymous client, interview applicants, refer candidates only when an exhaustive investigation of both applicant and client shows that they fit specifications. In order to function, these firms must create and keep contacts, and stay in the know. They are supported by fees from client companies on a yearly basis.

Women might begin as *secretaries* or *library assistants*. They abstract information from résumés and keep a card file of applicants, send data sheets to companies, run the office in the absence of their boss who is often traveling, work on graphic material for meetings. Some beginners, trained in psychology, may give and score vocational tests.

For Further Information about Jobs or Training

Public Personnel Association, 1313 East 60th Street, Chicago 37, Illinois

XVII

PHOTOGRAPHY

As a child, you were given your first camera at an early age and learned to make pictures indoors and out by the time-exposure method, flashbulb, fast lens. You found what made a good picture, how to snap moving objects, the effect of facing into the sun. You knew enough optics to realize why that box camera never had to be focused since the pinhole lens brought all images to the same focal point regardless of distance. As you grew up, you experimented with printing and developing in a makeshift corner, made enlargements for friends, took candids at their parties; you contributed photographs to the school paper, went from class to class with camera in hand, and showed that you meant business.

IF YOU WANT TO TURN A HOBBY INTO A CAREER, become an *apprentice* to a photographer you admire. You will keep the appointment schedule, mix hypos, wash prints, scale negatives, answer the telephone, clean up the darkroom equipment, run errands, observe. Or as a *secretary* in a portrait studio, you can arrange lights, assist with poses, help to relax the subject, suggest becoming costumes, accessories, backgrounds, do enlarging, reducing, retouching, coloring. The secretary on a newspaper may get her first break at a flower show or a reception. And she may get orders besides.

On your own time, take pictures of events in your town: the whale that was washed ashore, the modernistic church that is attracting attention, an optical illusion. If nothing newsworthy seems to happen, try out an original idea: a series of photographs to prove your theory that people look like their dogs and their cars. Consult photographers. Get in touch with editors. Do your own selling.

Lucinda W was an avid photographer all through school. She never stopped. Because she attended every event, she continually had pictures of things her classmates wanted: a county fair, scavenger hunt, engagement party, firehouse fire. That meant orders which in turn meant recognition. As a result, when she graduated she had a collection of good examples of her work, a modest list of customers, even a price, which helped when she peddled her work to the local newspaper for assignments. She got them occasionally and a real estate office let her do photostats while she got her training.

The proof of your ability is in the candids you have taken, the assistance you gave magazine photographers who wanted campus shots for an article, your portfolio of photographs which shows your own style. Use your art background; let your sense of design come through; if you have a specialty, play it up. Show that you can *see*.

Try this. Look at a country scene or a group of city buildings: first count the number of shades of green; then concentrate on finding *lines;* next look for *forms,* apart from color and line; notice how each time you change your objective, different things seem to jump out. A good photographer has strong and individual powers of observation.

ABOUT TRAINING.   You don't have to go to college, but *do*. And visit museums, study paintings, while you are taking photographic courses. You need to be artistic, have manual dexterity, be able to see, feel, think, and have something to say.

BUSINESS CONSIDERATIONS.   Some states require a license for commercial photography; some cities and towns have further requirements. Learn the laws: you may not photograph money, copyrighted material, visas; a newspaper may print a person's picture in a news story, but not in an advertisement without his permission.

As a business, photography is expensive. Equipment comes high, perhaps more than you will make in a year. At the start, you must keep your own records, set up a file system to know what you have taken and where it is, do your own bookkeeping.

As an occupation, it is a complete one-woman operation. You work independently, have the ideas, do the research, photographing, editing, reworking, and selling. It often involves travel, is lonely.

You may take pictures for advertising, fashion, feature stories, science, medicine (photomicrography: pictures taken through a microscope). Or you may specialize in portraits, for which you need patience and tact. Throughout it all, you must keep up your enthusiasm and interest.

For Further Information about Jobs or Training

American Society of Magazine Photographers, 1472 Broadway, New York 36, New York

XVIII

PUBLIC RELATIONS AND
FUND-RAISING

PUBLIC RELATIONS

Public relations, the Misunderstood Betsy of Madison Avenue, is usually defined by tossing it back and calling it relations with the public. Yet it is more than that. Its role is to make these relations *good* ones. Therefore, it is the whole process of putting and keeping a company, idea, or person in a favorable light with all its publics: customers, employees, stockholders, the community.

The layman often thinks of the term loosely as referring to parts of a public relations program: the policy of answering all mail the day it arrives; the corsages given to customers on the opening of a new restaurant; the man whose only function is to greet newcomers.

Public relations is not, as some people mistakenly think, a succession of cocktail parties on the expense account or a pleasant gathering of people for discussion.

A total PR plan includes: studying what people now think of a company, formulating a continuing policy to get the public to think well of it, and carrying out that policy. While it is used as a device to try to correct a poor impression—to assure the public that flying is safe, despite a plane accident—

a sound program will encompass that assurance at all times, not only in an emergency.

PR differs from advertising because it is often not apparent and is aimed at more than just potential buyers.

HOW DOES PR WORK? Through deeds, and through the spoken and written word, used to tell a story—about the quality of a service or to sell an idea. Writing is the important technique involved, but the total ability needed is more than this. Public relations today is being removed from the technician class and put into the policy-making one. Therefore, logical thinking and the ability to see a total picture and come to appropriate conclusions are vital.

PERSONAL AND EDUCATIONAL QUALIFICATIONS. Potential writers may consider going into PR provided they get along with their fellow men, but the gregarious won't qualify if they can't express themselves. Researchers will be interested, as well as those who want to work with their hands.

A smart job hunter will be a joiner (in school or college she will have belonged to many clubs and taken part in student activities); she makes a good presentation on paper as well as in person; her approach is tactful and planned (she'll be sure about getting appointments lined up ahead of time); her résumé is attractive (naturally it is well composed); her letters are as brief as a busy employer would want, and she is thoughtful in making them easy to answer (the enclosed postcard approach); she knows how to follow up her interviews. In short, she will treat her job hunting as she would a public relations campaign.

After you have been on the job long enough to know that you like the field and want to stay in it, then special courses may be indicated. How will you know? To be successful in public relations you should be: continually good-natured, not unattractive, able to give people a feeling of confidence in your opinion, able to maneuver them without their knowing it, outgoing but not overpowering, and capable of leading while remaining in the background.

Those additional courses might be economics, fund-raising, journalism, public relations, publicity, psychology, statistics, writing. Take them for a reason; in themselves they are not door openers to a job or a career.

HOW TO BEGIN.   The likely way to start is as a *secretary* either in the PR department of a company, or with a firm that does public relations for other companies, or for non-profit organizations or free-lance PR men. Some June graduates are able to start with only typing as their skill if they have had a wealth of summer office experience. For research, you can go in as an *interviewer, coder,* or *tabulator.*

Secretaries might clip newspaper items for a publicity scrapbook; send releases to newspapers about mergers, annual meetings, the opening of a branch store; circulate notices within the company; keep mailing lists up to date (address changes, press contacts); proofread correspondence, speeches, reports.

WRITING IS YOUR AIM.   If you have had experience in your college publicity office as an undergraduate, you might be able to start as a *writer* for a house organ, interviewing employees for items in the news and notes column; or as an *editorial assistant* who proofreads and rewrites articles to fit space in a professional journal; or as a *correspondent* in the reader-mail department of a magazine, sending form answers to run-of-the-mill questions, or composing individual answers to unique queries.

You should be able to think on the typewriter (longhand won't be fast enough for you), turn out *and* recognize good copy. Your eventual productions might include brochures about a company; articles for an employee magazine; write-ups of executive appointments for the papers; feature stories about a new product; speeches for the president to give at a convention; interim progress reports; picture captions. This writing won't be the college thesis type; much of it is promotional, lively, sometimes staccato. You also proofread and revise your own copy or rewrite articles submitted by others. Most of the writing is anonymous. PR is like ventriloquism: your voice does the work someone else gets credit for. Later, your title might become *editor, general writer, feature writer,* or *director of publicity.*

Researchers supply information for writers. They unearth data and study the potential market of a product through their knowledge of resources. They may interview customers for testimonials, or go through old annual reports to collect historical facts for a special anniversary celebration.

THOSE WHOSE FORTE IS PEOPLE set up association meetings, working with members, speakers, hotels, and airlines. They arrange press interviews or television appearances for a recently elected officer of a company or a newly published author of a book. This means knowing whom to get in touch with, what approach to take—telephone, letter, or in person— the areas the press and television media specialize in, the right timing. They represent the company at luncheons and are ready to answer questions or give a speech if called on. They schedule events such as press parties, convention exhibits, contests.

The artistically or mechanically inclined find satisfaction doing production, designing booklets, arranging layout, selecting type faces—Garamond for a professional association, Gothic for a bank—choosing photographs and cropping them to size. They draw up announcements of public appearances or fashion shows. A knowledge of proofreading symbols and of printing are in order, besides an understanding of reading habits. *Photographers* take pictures for posters, news stories, booklets.

WHAT IS YOUR PR FUTURE? The titles ahead of you might be: *public relations counselor* (in a firm which handles public relations for other companies), *speaker* (who represents a person or a political party and addresses groups to enlist their votes), *director of public relations* (head of that department in a corporation), *account executive* (who plans and works out campaigns for clients of a PR firm), *vice president* or *president* (of a company or of a public relations firm).

Women have gone far in this field in spite of continued prejudice. You can safeguard your future by specializing in a subject that is typically a woman's domain, but you don't have to. More important than a specialty is mental flexibility. A public relations firm must be able to jump from one account to another and bone up on the background needed for very different assignments—whether it be a campaign to inspire confidence in a frozen food after erroneous reports of poisoning from it, or the planning of a circus parade.

As far as job stability is concerned, it is a somewhat fickle field. Public relations firms continually gain and lose accounts. It is a service which people may dispense with during a recession. Starting salaries are normal. The top of the scale is as high as you are able to make it.

The jobs are found in manufacturing firms, shops, public utility companies, professional associations, labor unions, and PR consulting firms. Almost every business center has its quota of PR: New York, Los Angeles, Washington, Philadelphia, St. Louis, Pittsburgh have leaders in the field. In general, the hours for beginners are regular, but may involve overtime to meet newspaper deadlines or as responsibilities increase. This field is probably growing faster than any such service group.

FUND-RAISING

Fund-raising is the pursuit of the philanthropic dollar, and because this pursuit has become so hot, the art of fund-raising is now big business. Partly as a result of new promotional techniques and the tax-deductibility of gifts, $8,700,000,000 were given to public causes by private sources during 1961.

Fund-raising is the process of getting complete support for organizations that are fully dependent on voluntary gifts—adoption services, social welfare agencies, health groups, and the like—or partial support for those whose dues do not pay for their work—universities, museums, churches, hospitals, public libraries.

Success in fund-raising depends on effective public relations. Fund-raisers must be well versed in the principles of public relations.

HOW FUND-RAISING WORKS.   If a school wants to raise money for scholarships or faculty salaries, the fund-raising firm studies the curriculum and administration; goes over the financial statements; notes how much was raised in previous years; examines the list of donors, the size and number of gifts; sees how strong the alumnae group is, how active the board of directors, how well informed they are kept; determines the attitude of the community; in short, estimates the chances of attracting the money needed and then prepares a written case showing why the institution deserves support.

Then the firm does the steering. It draws up a plan, decides what groups to approach (business, foundations, parents), establishes a schedule, organizes committees of volunteers, shows them how to develop special projects like theatre benefits, house tours, art shows. The actual asking for money is done by the board and volunteers, not the paid staff. The fund-raiser works behind the scenes and pulls strings, while others perform on stage.

HOW TO GET STARTED AS A FUND-RAISER.   A general liberal arts background plus a good sense of PR form the best preparation. Beginners may be *typists* or *secretaries,* and they move up fast if they are alert. They type appeals, foundation presentations, acknowledgments, make notations of receipts, compile information about individuals to be approached, watch society columns for announcements, notify the papers about teas, meetings, large gifts received.

As a secretary, you might work at the office of the firm handling the acount, or at the organization itself, serving as liaison between the two. You set up the office, keep records, see that directions are understood, carry them out.

Valerie T started as a typist for a PR firm. She soon demonstrated her mind for details and understanding of the importance of accurate records. Every day before she got to the office she read the morning newspaper and made a note of marriages, divorces, or of company moves that affected mailing lists. Twice she read obituaries of people on the list to be solicited that day, and she caught the letters before they were mailed. Her thoroughness brought her rapid promotions, and at the end of a year she was transferred to another city and put in charge of a campaign there.

You don't have to begin as a secretary if you can write; you might work on publicity, draft printed pieces, descriptive leaflets, news releases; perhaps design letterheads and receipts; go over current catalogues for possible improvement.

Volunteer work is a good entree because many *volunteers* are needed. When you show what you can do, you might work into a paid job. Volunteers shake canisters, distribute programs at a ball, do clerical work for a theatre benefit (draw up lists, send announcements, persuade their friends to subscribe, assign seats, mail tickets).

SUITABILITY FOR WOMEN. This is a field for women because of their interest in education and welfare and the arts. Those in charge of a fund-raising program may be called *director of public relations* or *of fund-raising, financial* or *fund-raising secretary,* or, in the more euphemistic and modern version, *director of development* or *public interest officer.* For women advanced jobs are apt to be on the staff of the organization raising the money, rather than with a firm, chiefly because firm operations move from town to town. Some women are free-lancers and move from account to account.

Many women are board members who have developed a high degree of skill at raising money. Their function is to go directly to those who have money or influence. They visit prospects, ask theatre managers for a benefit, make speeches, entertain potential donors. Some of them have stepped into paid fund-raising jobs. Others have contributed their time as fund-raising counsel for their favorite charity. Mrs. M organized and ran three drives for her college, at intervals of ten years. She raised several million dollars, besides saving the college considerable expense from fees.

Fund-raising is a seasonal business. People at the beach aren't receptive to appeals; therefore drives are confined to winter months. This means long vacations for the free-lancers, and time for preparatory work on next autumn's campaign for others.

Salaries for beginners are average; those for the experienced are good; the free-lancer can do very well.

For Further Information about Jobs or Training

American Alumni Council, 1707 N Street, N.W., Washington 6, D.C.

American College Public Relations Association, 1785 Massachusetts Avenue, N.W., Washington 6, D.C.

Public Relations Society of America, Inc., 375 Park Avenue, New York 22, New York

The American Association of Fund-Raising Counsel, 500 Fifth Avenue, New York 36, New York

The American Public Relations Association, 1427 I Street, Washington 5, D.C.

XIX

PUBLISHING

Scratch the ambition of most college seniors and you find a publishing house, magazine, or newspaper. It is interesting to speculate on the reason. Perhaps it results from the encouragement of a well-written thesis, or the familiarity with books after a lifetime of study, or the comfort of a vital medium of communication between members of the gregarious race. Before you commit yourself to this field do some soul searching to be sure your interest is real.

Publishing is the business (repeat: business; not only the art, profession, and service) of obtaining material, working on it, getting it printed, informing the public that a publication is ready, and selling it.

Those who like to read, teach, do research, use a foreign language, write, work with people, free-lance, can find opportunities in publishing, even in unexpected areas of the field.

Beginning jobs for *bookkeepers, clerks, receptionists, secretaries, stenographers, typists* occur throughout the field. A high school education will suffice, but for the most part college training is needed if you want to keep rising.

BOOKS

Making a book consists of getting a manuscript, editing it, designing and manufacturing the book, selling and promoting it, and keeping financial records.

This section deals with the many kinds of opportunities that await you in book publishing, but don't read it too literally. Publishing houses differ widely in the names they apply to various jobs, in the way job functions are assigned, and may even vary the duties from one kind of book to another.

FOR THOSE WHO LOVE TO READ.   Reading manuscripts is not like curling up with a good book and a box of candy. It is easy to read what you like, but in this business you must also read what you don't like, and then report on it.

On your first job as *secretary*, you might be allowed, during your lunch hour, to screen one of the manuscripts on that ceiling-high stack. Part of the reading job is simply a matter of sorting (a novel received by a textbook firm gets put on the return pile). Then you read to weed out the obviously unacceptable—those MSS which don't meet your company's writing and taste standards—and next write your comments.

You might also keep track of manuscripts that come in: make entry cards listing author, title, date of submission, and postage included. Or you might see visitors, set up conferences with authors and editors, and retype revised pages. Most manuscripts are unsolicited; most are rejected. Although a sampling can suffice, no manuscript is ever completely ignored; publishers always hope to find *that* novel.

A secretarial job might lead to one as *reader* or *assistant editor* in which position you consider further things in judging a manuscript. It may be good, but on a topic just published; or it may be similar to a book just out, and yet acceptable because it is on so popular a subject that there is still a market for it. Other considerations are the style, achievement of purpose, number of changes that will have to be made, length therefore cost, probable lifetime. You can see that reading is more than reading.

As a manuscript reader, you must be able to skim. That does not mean reading superficially, but instead quickly and succinctly. See and take in only what you need, not every word. (The reading process consists of pausing on words in order to see them because our eyes are blind when they move. Prove this to yourself by looking at your eyes in a mirror, first at one, then at the other; you won't see them move.) A reader looks for general quality, not minute details. If you turn your head back and forth (like a tennis spectator) as your eyes go across the page, if you lip-read, or if your throat moves in accompaniment, you are a slow reader and should steer clear of this job. (Consider proofreading instead.)

FOR THOSE WHO WANT TO EDIT. An editor's work with an author may start as early as when the book is merely an idea; it continues through the final stages of publication. To be an *editor,* you need to have a teaching instinct—like to show people how to do things, encourage them to proceed on their own, cheer them on. Like the teacher, though, you must be interested in the pupil. Writing a book is a long, laborious process as well as fun; it looks easy to the audience after the polishing is done. Writers have peaks of achievement with every word a pearl, but they also have dead periods when they wonder where the next sentence is coming from. A primary requirement of a good editor is to understand that author-heartening comes before editing.

A *secretary to an editor* may have a fling at revising. Vera D's first job after college was secretary to a juvenile editor. She was allowed to make suggestions for reorganizing material, rewording, deleting, building up. The editor took it from there, adding her own changes and working with the author. After only a few months Vera D was telephoning employment agencies for her replacement: she had been promoted to editorial work.

IF YOU LIKE RESEARCH. *Copy editors, proofreaders,* and *indexers* are, in essence, researchers. A researcher is a person with intense curiosity: she loves to ferret, follow new trails, question everything, watch for discrepancies and contradictions, remember what she learns because it may be useful someday in another setting. She likes libraries, their hard chairs, their quiet, their noise, card catalogues, reference books. If this sounds like you, read on.

One kind of researcher uses an encyclopedia. She answers questions from readers who want more information. Another is a copy editor. She goes over the manuscript with an air of suspicion (if the hero in a period novel takes a pinch of snuff, she automatically checks to see if snuff was used in those days); she corrects footnotes, bibliographies, foreign phrases; makes the spelling, grammar, punctuation consistent. Her bible is the firm's style book that decrees what numbers are set in numerals, which written out; what words are hyphenated, spelled with two *l*s, italicized, taboo. She might prepare and check an index, if it is not done by the author or outside the firm. That means she must understand fully what she reads, keep both eye and mind on what she is doing, know which items are important to list, get them under the right headings. A page listed for Abraham Lincoln must not turn out to refer to the tunnel in New York or the city in Nebraska.

Augusta N, an editorial assistant, was given an author's bibliography to be sure the titles, names, and publication dates were correct. She went to the library for the answers, but made the mistake of working from the card catalogue rather than from the books themselves. As a result, typographical errors on the cards escaped her (such as the full names of publishers, easily spotted by an experienced copy editor); she later found how much she still had to learn.

Proofreading is another intensive job which can be a beginning one. Spend a day at the library with a proofreading manual and learn the symbols if you don't know them. A *proofreader* goes over the galleys (printers' proofs on long unpaginated sheets), watches for inaccuracies, is careful, reads slowly (it is easy to think a sentence is correct simply because it makes sense; yet a substitution of "not" for "now" can reverse the meaning). She will learn to check the proofs against the manuscript (sometimes with someone else reading the manuscript aloud to her). She needs to be thorough, mindful of details, able to do intensive work, see well, be more phlegmatic than flighty.

This paragraph shows how to indicate to the printer that a has been omitted, the type is out of line, one parenthesis (of an aside is reversed, lower case should be substituted for a Capital letter, space inserted between words, and a comma deleted.

Special editors are authorities on certain types of books or subjects: science, reference books, music. They frequently work from outside.

A special type of editing is coming in with books of programmed instruction. This new field originated with teaching machines. Programmed books present material to be learned in a certain form or program. This method of instruction is based on the principle that a person learns more efficiently and effectively if he is given information in small units, allowed to proceed at his own pace to make an appropriate response to each step, and then reinforced by being told the answer immediately after he has given his, instead of having to wait till his paper is corrected next week. The program is the initial learning experience in a subject area; it is not a review, drill, or test; new behavior is being created.

Under this system, questions of increasing complexity are presented. In one format a blank line is provided for the answer—the correct response covered by a slider. The student always has the chance to compare at once his response with the right one. In another format, the scrambled text, answers are given on separate pages from the questions; the reader is referred back to the original question-page if he gives the right response, to another for reteaching if he gives a wrong one. Here the items are generally those requiring a multiple-choice response.

Editors who have training in psychology work with authors or in programming centers. The field is still too new to have many jobs, but it is one to watch. Opportunities are increasing, but specialized training is required: hard to come by at this stage in the development of the field.

FOR APPLIED ART. The production department translates the wishes of the editor into the language of the printer. The *production manager* (usually a man) coordinates the designing and printing functions: estimating the cost of paper, printing, binding, illustrations, composition, manufacturing, plates; planning the schedule and seeing that it is met. The *art director* is responsible for the jacket and illustrations; the *designer* for the physical styling (layout, type face, paper).

The beginner in this area may be a *secretary, paste-up girl,* or *production assistant.* She learns how type face, paper, binding, colors are selected; how to experiment with layout, the principle of fitting a square picture into an oblong space (done by figuring from diagonals), how to make up dummy books (a cover plus a few printed pages for samples); she sees dust jackets and promotion pieces designed. If she is going ahead, she must know color separation.

Artistic ability is basic to the art production department, as is another discipline—arithmetic, for selection and decision depend on measurement. A production assistant estimates the number of pages a book will require by converting the elite or pica measurements of the typescript into ems of the printed page; selects the kind and size of type to fit. Cost enters in here: too many pages may mean an overpriced book; paper, binding, pictures, colors, and time are all cost items. It is necessary to know printing processes (offset, multilith, engraving); realize the problems involved (for instance, multiples of four pages are printed simultaneously on a large sheet, then cut; one extra page means three wasted; one kind of colored paper won't absorb ink, another weight can't be folded easily).

This department has an expediting function as well. It records manuscripts as they are received for printing, sets deadlines for each stage of production, keeps track of photographs to be used.

FOR PROMOTERS AND WRITERS.   The *subsidiary rights expert* is concerned with special sales. She deals with permission requests from authors to use her company's books, submits books for magazine or movie sales, reprints, book clubs. She keeps records, is in constant touch with the firm's lawyers concerning all agreements. She can work up from secretary. The promotion of books abroad is part of this department (if not of a special foreign department): answering requests for translation rights, watching international sales and the kind of material published by foreign companies. Here is a place for those who want to use a foreign language.

The *promotion director* promotes the book by supervising the writing of the spring and fall catalogues, jacket blurbs, flyers, announcements for trade journals, book clubs, salesmen, monthly newsletters, and by arranging for window displays and posters. Promotion is aimed at book dealers, libraries, and those who get books into the hands of the public.

The *publicity director* reaches the buying public directly, promoting the author in order to sell the book. An assistant in this department keeps the list of reviewers up to date, sees that they get copies of the book, that the newspapers have publication dates and biographies of authors; she arranges the mechanics of getting the author on radio or television, at a luncheon or autograph party. She learns how to write releases, deliver them and to whom, abstract quotations from advance reviews.

Advertising, which is concerned with all paid publicity, may be done in the publicity department or in a separate one. The *copywriter* selects the magazines, newspapers, trade journals in which the book is to be advertised; decides how much space is to be taken, when, and for how long; writes the copy or works with the advertising agency that does.

IF YOU LIKE SELLING. In bookstores you deal with the public, learn what books are popular with what kinds of readers, which prices acceptable, how tastes and interests change. A bookstore job can lead to one within a publishing firm.

Secretaries to sales managers of book companies keep track of salesmen's itineraries, take care of their requests (please mail copies of such-and-such books to the Blank Book Shop, one on approval to Professor This; type the list of prospects to be called on in That City); they send them flyers, galleys, pay checks. Or they may send out mail-order material to schools, colleges, libraries, and stores which want their shelves stacked with the latest books. Such a job can grow into publicity or selling—the bookstore rather than the door-to-door variety (except with special books like some encyclopedias that are not sold through bookstores).

Educational consultants, usually with teaching experience, supplement the work of those selling in the field. They demonstrate methods of teaching with certain books, attend conferences, set up convention exhibits.

The personnel department may suggest that job applicants read *Book Publishing* to understand the business, refer them to *Printers' Ink Directory of House Organs* and the *Literary Market Place* for names of other writing media and services, and *Publishers' Weekly* to be up on what different houses are bringing out. So many are drawn to this field that personnel interviewers emphasize the importance of knowing something about it before applying, and having office skills in order to do the work.

THE ARITHMETIC-MINDED who are not interested in production can find openings in the accounting department, one function of which is to keep track of advance royalties (paid before publication) and of the amounts due authors from sales related to their books.

A magazine is a publication that faces regular deadlines: weekly, monthly, quarterly. The pace is faster than in book publishing. More opportunities exist for staff writing: editorials, feature articles, notes, picture captions, promotion, answers to mail from readers. Secretarial work is the way in. Women are wanted at the top.

The *editor-in-chief* is in charge. She develops policy, selects and trains assistants, knows what her readers want, plans each issue, draws up the table of contents. The *managing editor* coordinates the work of the editorial department. *Special editors* manage individual departments: fashion, jobs, food, sports, news, international.

Secretaries make appointments for outside writers who want to discuss an idea for an article or sell a finished story; list the parties, lunches, conferences the editor should attend and remind her in time; arrange meetings to discuss future issues. Sometimes they can apply a special interest. In an interior design department, they might be given the assignment of rounding up furniture, curtains, rugs, books, wall decorations, or photographs to illustrate an article based on Mrs. Reader's questions about what to do with an inherited set of Louis XV furniture in her Frank Lloyd Wright house.

Secretaries may fall heir to tickets to ballets and concerts, in return for which they write reviews; route manuscripts, type them for the printer (an exacting job), or return them to authors, learn to read, edit. They may interview job applicants and keep employee files if there is no separate personnel department.

Editorial assistants, who may also have secretarial duties, might, on the instructions of the editor, call outside consultants for advice on a topic under consideration; get in touch with writers to do a feature; cover an exhibit, play, or opera; keep all editors apprised of plans, learn to copy edit, rewrite. If they, or secretaries, show a flair for writing, they may get a chance to do an article on a topic familiar to them, such as the students' attitude toward a campus problem.

Another opportunity to write is in the reader-mail department, responding to inquiry, praise, or blame. Some beginners start as secretaries, some as *correspondents* dictating answers into a machine. Experience with the subject of the magazine is sometimes required. A magazine for young women, who may ask questions about dressing, smoking, dating, may require its correspondents to have had camp, teaching, or group work experience.

The secretary in the advertising department helps compose salesmen's presentations; in publicity, she clips and files releases.

The production department has much scope and variety for artists. You start as a secretary or *paste-up artist*. Look at a magazine from the point of view of appearance. Notice the way each article begins: perhaps the first letter or word is capitalized; there may be no indentation, or an extreme one; or the article may start low on the page. See the size, kind, positions of the headlines; how the layouts of features, stories, editorials differ from each other (in books the chapters are consistent); study the placement of pictures and captions, the way lengthy text is broken up by subheadings, boxed information, illustrations, diagrams, changes in type. The production department makes these arrangements and also distributes the ads, decides on the cover. It also marks colors on proofs for the printer, figures prices, orders materials, sees that the magazine goes to press on time. With weekly news magazines the deadline is only days ahead, which means almost round-the-clock work for the last day or two; the editorial week might include weekends. With a monthly, the deadline may be three months off.

When there is a photography department, to picture models for a fashion story or business executives in a finance report, *prop girls* arrange bookings, watch for hard-to-find types of people, do secretarial work. They learn to assemble sets, track down accessories, have equipment built to order, keep note of borrowed items.

Research occurs in getting information for an article, listing the characteristics of a new reducing diet to be written up, or verifying statements in the first write-up of a news story done from an interview. Work in the statistical line includes surveying what readers want; dealing with all branches of the magazine and getting information from it; selecting names for questionnaires; tabulating, analyzing, summarizing results.

The function of the advertising department is to sell space. *Saleswomen* get in touch with prospective advertisers, arrange for them to take space, keep them informed of circulation figures, number of readers—not just of those who buy the publication, but the library public, friends, and those who read over shoulders. Secretaries keep lineage records of sales, make sure mailing lists are up to date, note personnel and address changes.

Magazines may be large and general, or geared to one group or subject. A great many are put out by individual groups: sorority magazines, company house organs, trade association journals. These publications are everywhere and offer good training in a wide range of duties and room to grow. Look into these while other applicants beat a path to the door of the slicks. As an editorial assistant, you might be assigned to the news and notes column, writing up what the members report about their new jobs or promotions. You copy-edit articles or conference papers, redraw diagrams, paste trial pages according to instructions, design a mimeographed sheet of reprints, distribute it, fill orders, list receipts, report when the supply runs low, total the number sold in a given time, and give an opinion about reprinting more.

Louise S left college after two years for financial reasons. She wanted to learn magazine work, and she got a job as a typist for an electronics journal. She was so thorough and accurate, and often showed such initiative and originality in experimenting with layouts, that she was made an editorial assistant in six weeks, and continued her education at night to insure her continued promotion. Knowledge of the field was not necessary; only her potential with words.

NEWSPAPERS

Newspaper publishing entails getting the story, reporting it to the office as fast as possible by telephone or in person, getting it written, rewritten, cleared, headlined, printed. A difficult field for women to enter, but they have done it. The place to begin is a suburban or small-town paper, as a *cub* (or *cub reporter*); for once, secretarial skills are not the pass-key, although shorthand and typing come in handy. A cub may be assigned to follow police routes or a fire engine, cover a garden club show, write obituaries, or report a speech. She must have an eye for news, a memory for detail (how many objects on a table can you name after only a few seconds of looking at them?), endless energy, a knack for turning up in time, strong feet.

There are other starting spots. A *copy girl* is virtually an errand runner, and run she does: news isn't news for long. She takes a story from desk to desk for various treatments, tears out after coffee for someone else, carries copy, soaks up the jargon, learns the technique and the pace.

An *editorial clerk* does checking (racing charts, stock market quotations, death notices), sees that lists are correct, names spelled correctly, data tabulated fully; she looks up information, types, may do a limited amount of writing, can become a reporter.

The *advertising telephone solicitor* calls advertisers to get them to take space for classifieds. A good telephone voice is the prerequisite. She is paid salary and commissions.

Those who write are: *reporters* (*legmen* don't write, merely telephone in the story); *rewriters,* who put a report into shape after it has been received, condensing without losing vital details; *stringers,* who cover the news in one particular area of a community and are paid by the inch; *columnists,* who specialize in one topic—finance, gossip, radio—writing daily or weekly columns; *correspondents,* experienced reporters who send news from distant places; *promotion writers,* who prepare copy for booklets, salesmen's data sheets, direct-mail advertising, posters, radio spot commercials, and who may also write ads for the corner drugstore or neighborhood grocer, and sometimes sell subscriptions.

Copyreaders, with the newspaper's style book always at hand, watch for errors, contradictions, boners, violations of taste or policy, possible libel; they rewrite articles to conform to the width and length of assigned columns, write headlines, indicate their size. Theirs is a desk job.

Newspapers use narrow columns and special type size to make the material easier to read. As an illustration

> Notice how much faster you can get through a paragraph set up like this one that you can read with fewer eye fixations and consequently more comfortably and efficiently than

one like this which extends across the page from margin to margin even though it consists of fewer units (letters and spaces) than the thinner column above.

Special editors are responsible for news and features on a particular subject (education, society news, real estate, sports); they coordinate the news, notes, and ads on their pages, assign reporters to concerts, art shows, house tours. Women's-page editing is often done in advance and is not necessarily a deadline job.

Research is sometimes done by the reporters and sometimes by others after the reports are turned in. It entails correcting statements, filling in dates, getting background material (the childhood of a national hero returning to his home town; the history of a bridge that has just collapsed). Since newspapers do more than gather and present news (they also exert pressure, uncover frauds, track murderers), *editorial assistants* do research for editorials, gather the facts to support opinions (statistics about automobile accidents, needed for a drive to get traffic lights installed, or the record of a government official the paper is endorsing for a coming election).

Promotion researchers provide figures for copywriters, coordinate market data, and dramatize selling points for sales and advertising departments; they must be highly accurate and have analytical minds.

Librarians keep files and clippings, are in charge of the morgue (newspaper parlance for a clipping collection), know where to find a photograph or biography in a hurry.

Artists design booklets and promotion pieces, draw charts, graphs, maps. If you are going to be a newspaper *photographer,* you must be a person who has a way of being there when things happen (the mine cave-in, the duck that stole a ride on a toy sailboat). You might start with photographic training or from a secretarial position on a newspaper or even from a writing job (if you have been dissatisfied with the pictures that have accompanied your stories). Newspaper photography is an active job, no office work.

The photographer shoots what the reporter at her side is noting. She must jump easily from the opening of the opera to a street accident or courtroom scene. She needs a tough skin. Few women are in this field, but those who are have made their mark.

The *purchasing agent* does all the buying, and must know how much to buy of what from whom and when. Experience in a printing firm, and a knowledge of the mechanics of typesetting, photoengraving, and stereotyping are the usual background.

The advertising department engages many women though the *advertising manager,* who gets the ads, is usually a man. *Advertising saleswomen* deal directly with clients and agencies, know the paper inside out, its circulation, its readership, to sell it as an advertising medium. They may work in any field, would probably do best in education, books, retailing. Many sell classified advertising by telephone or outside the office.

The circulation department gets the newspaper to subscribers, and works to increase circulation. The *circulation director* must be familiar with the mechanics of newspaper publishing, with marketing and promotion, as well as postal regulations and other effects on delivery. Telephone selling of home delivery offers many opportunities to women.

The *public relations director* is in charge of the events and functions promoted by the paper. Fashion shows, music festivals, collections for charity, camps for underprivileged children are all developed under her management.

What makes a good newspaperwoman? You must have many interests including a driving desire—and an ability—to express yourself on paper. You must be able to compose despite distractions. A fast clip with the typewriter and blue pencil will stand you in good stead. You read voraciously, but for pleasure and information, not escape. Perhaps you ran your own paper when you were 12; or you have been on your school paper or yearbook since, maybe even worked in the college publicity office. Courses in civics, economics, English, history, literature, the natural and social sciences are important, as, of course, is journalism, which some employers prefer to a liberal arts degree. You will live with pencil and paper in hand, have a growing vocabulary, a desk covered with dictionaries, thesaurus, reference books.

WHERE THE PUBLISHING JOBS ARE

Most book publishers are in New York, Boston, Philadelphia, though there are some in all the big cities.

Some book publishers deal only with trade books (fiction and non-fiction for the general public—adult or juvenile); some have school, college, and medical divisions; and even within the trade department there may be religious and business book divisions.

An important aspect of publishing, and an important outlet for jobs, is the *literary agent (authors' representative)* whose role is to find publishable books or articles, help authors with rewriting, select the houses or magazines most likely to be interested, represent the author in negotiations with the publisher. Agents may work as individuals, or with a firm. They are paid a percentage of the royalties from sales of the book, serials, articles, movie rights, foreign publications.

Jobs occur also with editorial services, which may do complete editing jobs for publishing firms, and with printing presses, and there may be opportunities in book clubs.

Magazines are published everywhere, the best known in big cities, the house organs wherever home base happens to be: Large Town, Texas—or Hamlet, Wyoming.

New York is the newspaper center, along with Philadelphia, Boston, and Chicago, but the job opportunities are with small city dailies, suburban sheets, Sunday editions, religious, union, ships-at-sea papers. Wire services cover places impossible for newspapers to reach, sending in news over wires. Syndicates carry puzzles, health columns, comics. The news-minded should remember that journalism encompasses also news magazines, radio, and television.

Most organizations have a publication of some sort. Many secretaries and executives are also editors or writers. Business firms put out employee newsletters, annual reports, instruction manuals, stockholder letters. Sometimes it is best just to get into a company that interests you, learn the business, and then apply your writing later.

Publishing generally pays less than many fields; starting salaries are low, but do go up. However, newspaper salaries are higher than in comparable work, and regulated by the American Newspaper Guild for its members; some papers pay more than the union requirements, plus overtime and various benefits.

Automation is taking over subscription departments, and other aspects of the newspaper business, but gathering and evaluating information is a job for man, not machine. Working conditions on newspapers are better than Hollywood makes them, and the work week is a normal one for regular employees.

For any publishing career you should have a respect for facts, your own growing library and a good one, an inquiring mind, intense curiosity, and a knack for remembering.

FREE-LANCING

Free-lance opportunities abound—usually for the experienced, but sometimes for the inexperienced who pass the tests. Copy editors, proofreaders, indexers, letterers, artists, photographers, translators, special readers are called in by book publishers. In addition, magazines use writers and cartoonists. Free-lance assignments special to the newspaper field are for crossword puzzle writers, book reviewers, stringers, space salesmen, columnists.

Mrs. D gave up a writing job when she married, then wanted to go back ten years later. She initiated a column on job information for an Illinois newspaper, although she lived in Massachusetts and worked entirely at home. Her column has become so successful that it has been bought by a syndicate and now appears in newspapers across the country.

A SPECIAL WORD FOR WRITERS-TO-BE

Before you set forth to become a writer you should know what kind of writing you want to do. If you want to try novels or short stories, then don't set forth at all, but stay home, work on your own time, and hope to interest a publisher when you have finished. If you want to write for a salary, that is another matter, as we have seen.

Consider doing your writing on the side, while you hold a non-writing job. Put off trying to apply full time to this skill until you are sure it is what you want to do. Sometimes the aura of the phrase "I am an author" deludes people into thinking that is what they want to be. Test it. Are you writing every spare minute, or protesting you haven't time? Time is seldom the problem. For years Mrs. E said she was determined to write. She did none after college, pushed it aside during her married years, then talked about it again when her children were grown. Finally, psychoanalysis disclosed that she never really wanted to write.

Writing is a tool that everyone should sharpen, and one that can bring satisfaction whether or not payment is attached.

For Further Information about Jobs or Training

American Book Publishers Council, 58 West 48th Street, New York 36, New York

American Newspaper Publishers Association, 750 Third Avenue, New York 17, New York

The Newspaper Fund, Inc., 44 Broad Street, New York 4, New York

XX

RADIO AND TELEVISION

Americans owned more television sets and even more radios (48,500,000) than they did telephones in 1960, and used them not only for entertainment. Through the medium of television classes have been taught on an island with a teacher shortage, the programs beamed by the Board of Education from the mainland; radios, as instruments, keep ships in touch with shore, railroad engineers with the caboose, police cars with headquarters, wives with their fishermen husbands. Even so, it is a tight field to get into.

If you can distinguish between radio-TV as entertainment and as an occupation, if you are willing to start on your home-town station, or begin and probably end as a secretary at a big-city network, then try it, with your eyes open. Opportunities for promotion at the networks are so scarce that the following discussion applies almost completely to non-network occupations.

Personnel interviewers at networks talk to more applicants than they can hire, are constantly forced to say, "You did well on your typing and shorthand tests, have just the qualifications we want, are suited to the job, but we have seen thirty others like you." They may suggest to a writer that she read the *Ross Reports,* a monthly publication that gives the names of producers looking for scripts, and the hows and wheres of submitting them. And they advise actresses to keep up with *Variety,* a newspaper of the stage, film, air.

Actresses, artists, musicians, writers, researchers have places in this field, but there is so much overlapping that no specialty always stands alone.

IF YOU WANT TO ACT. Acting on the air is a different process from on the stage, but the path is the same: long and hard. Study the medium, know the market for your talent. On radio, it is voice that counts. Test yours. You know that voices on tape or on the air sound differently from in person, especially a woman's. Be sure of your diction; a hiss comes over the mike faster than across footlights. Remember, before even thinking about working in the major radio and television centers, you must have experience, lots of it, at your local stations, either educational or commercial.

Announcers must be good actors, speak well, and have a wide knowledge of everything going on. A college degree is virtually required, a good vocabulary in English and sometimes in other languages, an understanding of acoustics, and the sound of conviction (each commercial should reflect enthusiasm). Announcers introduce programs, present material during intermissions, read news reports—and may suddenly find themselves in charge of a whole program. They work from a sheet that tells to the second when every item goes on, keep a log of what does take place, note omissions or time changes (the record is the basis of bills sent to sponsors and of checks sent to talent). They observe the special rules of their station (not giving the time at odd minutes like 3:37), are ready to pick themselves up after a fluff.

While the job of announcer usually goes to a man, there are women weather forecasters (*weather girls*) and sometimes women newscasters. And of course women frequently take part in commercials.

Sybil T was an actress who found an unexpectedly appropriate use of her ability with one of the networks in New York. Between Broadway roles she became a *tour guide*. She conducted groups through the studios and offices, explained how programs are put on, sound effects obtained. She learned her part, had to be ready to step out of it and speak her own lines when questions arose. She had a chance to use her sense of the dramatic, her knowledge of audience reaction. In fact, once or twice she became so histrionic that she was asked to stick more closely to her written speech.

IF YOU ARE AN ARTIST. Designing sets is the most obvious application of art training and the hardest to break into. It includes ordering furniture, selecting draperies and upholstery, supervising construction. *Costume designers* supply ideas for period pieces, know what colors and lines photograph well, which ones don't come across (this presented one set of problems in the old movies; color TV has brought another set). You must know when bare arms stand out, which kinds of silhouettes are bad, that black and white sometimes blur. A design major is needed for these jobs; department store work is good experience. In the major TV centers designing is a completely unionized job.

Make-up is a way in. Some graduates of beauty culture school specialize in TV; others have art school background. They learn what different lighting does to cosmetics, how to get someone to look younger or older, how to choose the right wig and meld it in with the natural hair, what to do for close-ups, even how to tone down a bright fruit jar or remove a highlight from a vase.

Photographers (probably men) in the publicity department supply newspapers and magazines with pictures of the network staff or personalities.

IF YOU WANT TO WORK WITH WORDS. Others in publicity write. Through accurate programs and feature stories they inform the public about forthcoming shows and the people who make them.

News itself comes in from *reporters* who stop at street corners, ball games, and airports, and broadcast on the spot or tape the event to play it back later (not telephoning it in, as in former days). It may also come in from newspapers or press services. This news may be rewritten, or read by the announcer right from the ticker. The writing must be informal, produced at a moment's notice ("we interrupt this program" has replaced the old-time Extra). Women have as hard a time getting into a radio's newsroom as they do a paper's.

Most staff writing is of continuity material, a tying-together process, supplying transitions between programs, wording the news, weather reports, music, interviews, introductions, closings.

In television, original scripts are in demand; existing material is being used up. Usually a free-lance job, TV scriptwriting involves a special technique, just as playwriting is different from short-story writing. Study scripts before you try any; find out which channels are looking for material, and how to submit it.

Radio employs *writers* for anecdotes, jokes, ad libs, not drama.

IF YOU ARE A MUSICIAN.   Those with graduate degrees start as *secretaries* to music directors, and collect music from stores, review it for suitability, test recordings for quality and length, set up and index the music library, type programs, file records, arrange classical and popular music in pleasing patterns. The *music director* makes the final selection of records, writes the accompanying script (whether it be an interpretation of a symphony or an introduction for a disc jockey), answers listeners' questions (from "What is the difference between the diatonic and chromatic scales?" to "Please settle an argument and tell me the name of the rock 'n roll played last night at ten o'clock"). Other advanced jobs are *junior producer, music researcher, copyright checker, pro-*

gram planner, music librarian. Television is on the lookout for original scores; these must be submitted with a script.

IF YOU LIKE RESEARCH. A guiding hand behind all this work is the *researcher,* who reports on the popularity of the programs, using the techniques of market research but facing the problem of invisible reaction (not as easy as tallying the number of books or cars bought). Networks have large research staffs which work with all departments and with audience rating services that measure numbers of listeners and viewers.

With the advent of television documentaries came jobs for another type of researcher—one with college training, funds of knowledge, and the ability to know where to verify information in a flash.

IF YOU ARE A JILL OF MANY TRADES. One of the most sought-after positions is that of *production assistant;* she is all things to her department. Pad and pencil in hand, she rushes from one instruction to another, chalks lines to show announcer, actor, soloist where to stand, goes out after coffee and sandwiches (which probably constitute dinner at 2:00 A.M.), prepares cue cards, sees that the right props are there or rounds them up, lends a belt or scarf of her own. Except in the major cities she might get a chance to operate lights or camera, help with make-up, even act.

If she goes ahead, and few women have along this line, she will have an all-inclusive job. The *program director (producer* or *director)* casts the show, arranges rehearsals, checks actors' stage business, clears the music, suggests and approves sets, orders art work, selects sound effects, gets the microphones properly placed, gives cues, supervises rehearsals, watches budgets, sees that the program gets on and off the air according to schedule, is ready to cut it if it runs over (she gets so she can *feel* ten minutes without glancing at the clock).

Women have been directors of women's programs. Stella

B, a former newspaper writer, conceived an afternoon radio program around the subject of people with interesting jobs. She set up the format, did sample interviews on tape, titled it "What People Do," and got a station to put it on as a sustaining (unsponsored) program. She spent most of her time finding subjects, interviewing and scheduling them. On the air she held informal discussions with teachers of the blind, aviators, professional golfers, drawing them out about their work, inserting her comments. After 15 years she retired, and because the program was popular, the station got another woman to take her place.

A radio *program coordinator* has a variety of duties, one of which is to line up people for interviews. She watches the papers for those in the news, famous names or those concerned with a topic of current interest (the first woman to be elected vice president of a local bank; the leader of a movement to stop a highway from being built through a park). Then she tapes an interview, probably not at the station, and the announcer retapes it so that his voice replaces hers. She watches hotel registers for the arrival of celebrities, is feted by publicity agents who are eager for her interest, creates her own show.

Production coordinators came in with *disc jockeys*. Deejays do more than put on and take off records (and some unions won't allow them to do that). They introduce, describe, comment; they read commercials, announce the time, give news reports, make related and unrelated comments. This total job is steered by the production coordinator who screens records, separates vocalists, sees that the style is different from that of other stations, resists pluggers from record companies and music publishers.

Continuity acceptance is a department special to radio and television. Its director screens advertising, entertainment, and reporting, to be sure it is in line with company policy, industry code, government regulations (some refuse liquor advertising or prohibit programs on drug addiction). Legal interest and background are appropriate here.

Some actresses, because of their outgoing nature, quick memory, realistic performance, are good at selling. Radio and television might use them in this capacity if they also have a head for business, either to get advertisers to sponsor an entire show or to take a few minutes between programs for a spot commercial to advertise their products. *Saleswomen* compete with those from other media, therefore must believe in their own and know its advantages. They work with researchers who tell them how many and what kind of listeners are where. They need tact and quick-wittedness (the sort they use to cover up when someone forgets his part) to explain why a commercial was omitted or an error made in a price quoted on the air.

FOR THOSE WITH A MIND FOR BUSINESS. Others with business leanings can work with the *business manager* (a man), who negotiates contracts with actors, pays salaries, sets up budgets for programs, and bills advertisers; or with the *operations network manager* (also a man), who organizes the physical process of getting programs to the public: orders the telephone cables that transmit shows to the studios, the cameras that photograph them; lists the time of each signal, pause, motion; and sees that everyone has a copy of the instructions.

WHERE TO FIND OPPORTUNITIES. In your job hunt, if radio or television is what you want, look for it at home; if the big city is your aim, apply for a job in another field. Remember, too, the other places that take part in this work: advertising agencies and package producers who put on entire shows for clients; services that pipe music to factories, restaurants, offices; foundations, church organizations, civic groups that have educational programs.

Big cities and small communities have broadcasting stations. The greatest number of employees are in New York, California, Illinois, Texas, Pennsylvania, and Ohio. Salaries are average to low. Many unions are involved with the networks and so each person's network job is carefully delineated, whereas at a local station you might be able to do several different jobs.

Radio and television are media used to a great extent by those not on their payroll, and you may find the chances of your getting on the air are better if you are an employee in another kind of business—members of political or public service organizations are frequently invited to appear on radio and television.

TRAINING YOURSELF. A good background for this field is whatever will help you prove you know what you are talking about when you express a desire to go into it. Ask for work with camera, mike, booms, lighting at your college radio station; try campus dramatics, summer stock, little theatre groups. Show that you are versatile, have ideas. But remember, this does not mean you are trained—only informed.

Radio today is being geared to people on the move (from room to room or house to house); to times when you can't watch television but can listen to your transistor. The trend is toward quick changes to hold attention and stop people from flipping the dial. Local stations offer services to keep housewives tuned in. One in Maine has a program called Open Mike: anyone may have two minutes on it—a boy looking for a hay-pitching job, a farmer with a horse to sell, a mother wanting to express her opinion about school taxes. Suggestions for other attention-getters can pave your way.

You should be able to take unpredictable variety, stiff competition, and temperamental coworkers who do not allow *you* to be temperamental. And you should like erratic hours, last-minute changes, and the kind of pressure that requires you to stay within time bounds and finish on the nose.

For Further Information about Courses and Training

American University and Northwestern University have internships conducted under the auspices of the Educational Foundation of The American Women in Radio and Television.

Other colleges and universities have similar programs.

XXI

REAL ESTATE

Real estate is a business for those who are interested in living arrangements, decorating, selling, finance—and for those who like physical excercise.

TRAINING QUALIFICATIONS. Maturity is in your favor. Formal education is not mandatory, but the more schooling you have, the better. It helps to take courses in real estate, and study some psychology: you will need understanding and humor, and the patience to listen to other people's problems.

GETTING STARTED. Secretarial work is a good beginning, as is experience in the record department in a real estate office. Here you learn about changing values, and see the bookkeeping behind buying and selling property. After you have worked for a broker, you may take the examination for saleswoman. Two years of selling are required before you are eligible for a broker's (agent's) license.

A *saleswoman's* job consists of showing houses to clients and answering questions about prices, taxes on property, how to get a mortgage, expected changes that may affect values (a new highway to be built close by); nearness to schools, shops, public transportation, railroad station; snow removal; zoning regulations (a family with two children may not be allowed to buy a house with only two bedrooms); the direction in which the town is growing (one man may be after an isolated piece of property because he hopes its surroundings will be built up in a few years and thereby increase its value; another may want the land only if it is likely to remain isolated). Besides showing houses, you watch newspapers for listings of properties, and keep up with the market.

You must be able to read blueprints, estimate room sizes by taking a quick look at them, walk up and down stairs of unfinished houses, negotiate sales, arrange compromises. Pay is on commission.

And you have to be able to take a near miss. Constance F, a real estate saleswoman in Florida, showed a house to a man who liked it and gave every indication of wanting to buy it. She thought she had the sale in the bag. He did buy the house, but then told her he had been negotiating with the owner before she had shown it to him. Lost: one $2,000 fee.

Your constant reference is the manual of the Real Estate Board of your state. It includes: commission tables, rules for appraisals, methods of measuring floors—allowing for columns or air vents, advertising regulations (beware of superlatives; draw furniture to scale so as not to be misleading about space).

BIG-CITY OPPORTUNITIES. You can act as *rental agent* for an apartment house or business building, but jobs in cities are becoming more complex. You will have to understand the complicated transactions, tax features, and corporate setups of cooperatives (apartments which are owned, not rented). Residential real estate in small communities is a simpler and more likely area for women.

As a woman, you know what characteristics to watch for in a house: number of closets, location and sizes of rooms, heights of children's windows, convenience of kitchen oven. Your ability to sell increases with your knowledge of the area —What will grow in this soil? Are the neighbors quiet? Where does the water come from?—and so you will find more prospects who have confidence in you in your own neighborhood.

Saleswomen work for *brokers* who, besides selling, also may appraise and manage property, arrange for loans to finance sales, advise on the use of the acreage (should this land be turned into a farm or divided into lots and rented?).

This business is highly competitive; other salesmen, everybody's friends, the client himself, and Dame Chance are competing with you. You must be a quick, clear thinker, emotionally stable and shrewd: know when you have what a client wants, or hold him at bay until you do. You can enter this field at any time during your life, engage in it full time or part time, or take it up after retirement.

For Further Information about Jobs or Training

National Association of Real Estate Boards, 36 South Wabash Avenue, Chicago 3, Illinois

XXII

TELEPHONE

Women comprise 60 per cent of all telephone workers, and are predominant in every department except those concerned with construction, installation, and maintenance. A high school education is preferred; usually aptitude and ability tests are given.

The dial system has made the old-time telephone heroine obsolete (the country central who knew Dr. A was setting Mr. B's broken leg, and waylaid him to report about the boy who had swallowed the cleaning fluid); but it has brought new heroines: small children left alone have dialed the operator and reported a fire which she traced by locking the call.

The *operator*'s job today is more varied than when the work consisted of handling calls at a switchboard. Now that the majority of customers can dial not only local but long-distance points, most telephone operators are assigned to Information service or to calls the user cannot complete himself: person-to-person, reversed charges, credit card. Others record numbers of customer-dialed long-distance calls, look up routes and rates, or complete local calls in the few places where dial telephones are not in use.

Operators need good health, good enunciation, manual

dexterity, spelling and arithmetical ability, tact, reasoning, and a helpful attitude.

Office jobs include *clerks* who make out bills for calls (from special equipment which records them or from operators' tickets), do filing, bookkeeping, statistical work, and maintain records. *Stenographers* and *secretaries* answer letters, type orders for service or booklets that teach people how to answer the telephone clearly and use it efficiently; some work with data-processing equipment that tallies calls; others are counter and mail tellers.

Service representatives, for which some companies prefer college training, act as liaison between customers and the company. Working at a desk which is half file drawer containing records of telephone users in a given area, they deal with the public by telephone. This job is for those who want to work entirely with people: no office skills are involved. Representatives recommend and sell services, route requests for the installation of color telephones, dials that light up, controls that increase volume for the deaf, or a service that enables conferences to be held between people in several cities; they take orders for telephones to be turned off during vacation, explain bills and company policy, arrange payments on account, note address changes. They must absorb and remember a wide range of information, express themselves well, have infinite patience, be able to soothe angry customers, look up numbers quickly, do several things at once.

Supervisors, usually women who work up from other jobs in the company, stand by ready to answer difficult questions, listen in while service representatives are being trained, oversee the work.

College graduates with mathematical aptitude are hired as *programming trainees* to work with the data-processing equipment that is making telephone service automatic.

Telephones are becoming more prevalent with those on the go. Taxis use them to avoid doubling back on their tracks;

businessmen in car or plane keep in touch with home or office; vacationers on train or private yacht may be reached at once. Cables that carry radio and television programs across the country are leased from telephone companies; messages, photographs, TV programs are beamed around the world via satellite.

JOB PROSPECTS.   Salaries are normal; benefits good. Working conditions are also good, though operators' hours may include night or split shifts, and their work may become intensive after a while. The jobs are with some 3,000 telephone companies in the United States, and the industries that have switchboards (PBX or private board exchange). While technological advance is replacing some of the clerical work, increased demands for more telephone services are bringing job openings, and people are still the backbone of the industry.

XXIII

TRAVEL

You can travel in three ways: on vacation, on a job, vicariously. If wanderlust is really in your blood, then it should not matter what the job is. Vivian B is one to whom travel means more than the daily work. Nearing 50, she has had a simple clerical job with an airline for 20 years, the pay is low, and she is not trying for advancement; she has what she wants: no responsibility after five o'clock, weekends for travel, worldwide vacations.

Many a young job hunter has yearned for an occupation on wheels or in the air, while her older friends wished their jobs (not in a travel business) did not keep them on the road so much. The demands and discomforts of travel can seem great. When you travel for fun, you name the place and pace. Not so when you do it on salary. You pack and unpack several times a week; eat in all kinds of restaurants or roadside stands, with large numbers of people or alone, or have your entire sequence of meals upset when a jet takes you into a new time zone or new day; you get varying amounts of sleep, seldom enough; must convert dollars into pounds, guilders, rupees, ticals; submit to climate changes; then come home to find your desk piled so high you can't catch your breath even then.

Consider these before you let the lure of the far-away color your job choice.

AIRLINES

Since the days of Icarus, man has dreamed of flying. Balloonists of the eighteenth century and the Wrights of the nineteenth made it possible. In the twentieth, Superman carried our imaginings even farther; the astronauts turned these into reality.

Today, women as *airline stewardesses* (or *hostesses*) hold jobs in the air. Theirs is one of the most sought-after occupations (*Mademoiselle* sells more reprints of its article on airline hostesses than any other). College background or experience is preferred. They must meet requirements of minimum age, eyesight, maximum height, looks (employment interviewers come right out and tell them if they are not pretty enough), grooming, poise; they must be unmarried, and nice to everyone. Exact specifications vary with the company.

An airline stewardess is a welcomer, nurse, waitress, comforter, public relations representative, saleswoman. Her job begins ahead of time, for she is on call. When she gets to the airport, one hour before scheduled departure, she sees that enough food and beverages are in the galley, helps passengers with light luggage, gets the names of people listed to be on her plane, notifies the dispatcher about those who do not appear. When the plane takes off, she greets passengers over the public address system (in several languages on an international flight), instructs them in fastening seat belts. Airborne, she answers questions of inexperienced or hardened fliers (what is that city, how are clouds formed, why are there air pockets?). She serves food, heats bottles, gets pillows, regulates temperature and ventilation, keeps the plane tidy, explains customs procedures, maintains calm during emergencies. When the flight is over she makes a report on the number of

passengers, condition of the cabin, quantity of supplies. She
is on her own; no supervisor sees that she does her job. She
represents the airline and is responsible for its standing with
the public; if people like her, they will like the company.

TRAINING, which she can get at a school through which some
airlines recruit (better check with the airline before signing
up), or in a course with the company, consists of the history
of aviation, meteorology, navigation, schedules, theory of
flight, first aid, how to handle passengers (those who are
frightened and those who want a date); she goes through drills
on what to do in case of forced landing; one line teaches her
to take pictures so she can give photography tips to passengers.

Airline work is not only an outlet for those who like people
and travel, but also for the rare mechanical girl who likes
heavy industry rather than delicate instruments. Martha C
applied for a publishing job after college because she thought
it was the thing to do, but confessed she really wished she
could continue her summer job as garage helper. She had
washed windshields, filled gas tanks, changed oil, tested tires,
polished cars, but she knew that was no permanent place for
a woman. Her vocational counselor suggested a stewardess
job. She applied for one and got it, delighted to be so near
the mechanics of transportation.

If a stewardess wants to advance she might become *school
instructor, chief stewardess, employment representative,* or
she might go into sales, public relations, or advertising, or
marry a passenger.

She wears a uniform, has all expenses paid when away from
base; may be allowed flights on company planes and reduced
rates abroad, as are all employees. She probably lives in or
near a city that has a base. Salaries are good; hours per month
are few (usually around 85) but can be extensive per flight if
the plane cannot land at its scheduled airport; most stewardesses belong to a union.

But all the glamour is not gold. Frances T had what

sounded like the ideal, exotic job, but she was not happy about it. She worked only three days a week for an international line that left four footloose days. No other employer wanted her for these days, since they varied and might come on weekends. Her job took her to Paris one week, London the next; she traveled on a special plane for executives only, met interesting people, stayed at the best hotels when away from home. But she found her life disjointed, and worried about her tendency toward becoming blasé. When she had dinner with her friends in other businesses and discussed what they had done that day, her casual "I went to Bermuda" sounded contrived. She stayed a stewardess for three years, the average length of time, and then left to marry.

Weigh these contrasting points in considering the future of the field: the job is popular, yet about 40 per cent of the stewardesses resign yearly; the field is expanding, but requirements are stringent; airlines do not easily find qualified applicants, but faster jets mean fewer stewardesses needed.

Square it with your family. If they are not air-minded or just don't want you up there, there are other jobs:

In airline offices are *secretaries, teletypists,* and *radio operators* (though not often women) who send pilots messages about weather conditions. *Reservation* (or *ticket*) *agents* deal with the public, answer questions about hours and connections, sell tickets. Other clerks work behind scenes from diagrams of the planes, noting names, addresses, telephone numbers of passengers, making sure the same seat is not sold twice. These jobs are not nine-to-five, but in shifts, a year's schedule being made out in advance, so you know today what you will be doing on December 25. Usually the shift change is gradual, not alternating days and nights.

Electronic data-processing machines are doing much of the work of relaying, recording, and producing information and tickets.

Many of the secretaries and ticket agents who are college

graduates move into supervisory jobs; at least one has gone into programming.

GOVERNMENT WORK

The Federal government and the United Nations offer jobs for civilians abroad. Beginners go as *secretaries;* others must have solid experience in their field: *nurses, home economists, teachers, researchers, writers, nutritionists, physical* and *occupational therapists, laboratory technicians.*

Some outlets are: ICA, International Cooperation Administration, which helps foreign countries develop scientific techniques (modern food processing, inoculations); UNESCO, the United Nations Educational, Scientific, and Cultural Organization, which tries to raise literary and living standards; the Food and Agricultural Organization, which attempts to increase the production and consumption of food all over the world by studying diets and teaching underdeveloped countries better ways of planning, preserving, preparing food; WHO, the World Health Organization, which helps people achieve the highest levels of health; the Foreign Service of the Department of State, where three-fifths of the staff positions are held by women, in clerical and secretarial jobs, usually starting in this country before being sent overseas.

TRAVEL AGENCIES

If the idea more than the fact of traveling appeals to you, then you may prefer to get other people under way while you stay at your desk. But travel agency work does not consist simply of discussing the beauties of the Alps or the fascinations of the African bush. Although your own travels will help you get a job, these are lagniappe to the agencies which look first for hard, down-to-earth clerical ability. It is not enough to know the particular spot on the Jasper Highway where you take that climb for the view of rare green Peyto Lake, or how to reach that obscure spot in India by elephant.

You start as a *secretary* or *typist* (unless you have reservation work behind you). You write letters, type itineraries, fill out mile-long tickets and make sure they are right (no inserting the name of an airline that does not take that route), look up alternative resorts when a company is on strike, file folders of hotels and tours, interpret timetables which may be in Navy terms, mesh schedules.

Travel representatives, who hold the job you probably want, work out trips by plane, bus, ship, tying in the reservations with hotels, resorts, camps. They describe the climate, people, food, what to wear, see, avoid. Customers may be young vacationers with simple requests, experienced travelers with complicated demands they change after the trip is booked, or business executives who must cover certain ground and hit certain spots on given dates. Travel agencies show what places to omit to save money, how to take another route and save miles. Sometimes their knowledge of their tools is more helpful than someone else's knowledge of roads and speedometers. Beatrice M had a job during the war in the transportation office of a firearms plant. Since gasoline was rationed, this office approved the workers' applications for ration tickets—distance from the plant determining the number of tickets. One day a company executive filed an application and reported that he lived ten miles away. Beatrice M told him it was only eight. He argued that he had clocked the distance. She rolled her measurer across a map and proved to be right; she had seen a different route from the one he had been taking.

Travel agents sell on commission: from the carriers and hotels they represent, plus, often, a small fee from customers. Hours are long, frictions frequent; prosperity is tied up with the economy. They may visit the resorts they represent, and try new ones as well, to solicit business.

JOB OPPORTUNITIES occur also with companies which have their own travel departments; in passenger departments of transportation companies (a railroad will help you make out a whole trip); with automobile associations; the travel sections of magazines; oil companies that maintain the latest automobile maps showing road construction, bridges washed out; government agencies which want to encourage international visitors; state tourist officers and chambers of commerce which send information to out-of-state inquirers or answer the questions of those who want to know where are good vacation spots, inexpensive inns, warm swimming.

Many women work in the travel field. Their patience, perseverance, ability to work long and hard, respect for accuracy, interest in other people's plans are what got them there.

For Further Information about Jobs or Training

American Society of Travel Agents, Inc., 501 Fifth Avenue, New York 17, New York

National Association of Travel Organizations, 1422 K Street, N.W., Washington 5, D.C.

XXIV

THE RETURNER

The 1950s saw the arrival of the returner, the woman who had left work to raise a family, and now, with her youngest child in school, wanted to come back to a paid job. In some cases she had never worked before, but the term still held. Actually she was the same person who had always been applying for part-time jobs, but now she had a name and a spotlight.

Suddenly volumes were written about her, explaining her, cheering her. Writers delved into sociology books and came up with observations about our changing mores, woman's role, early marriages, education not finding an outlet in the kitchen, household short cuts bringing more free time.

Women themselves said they wanted to use their minds, get in the swim, be paid for what they did, spend the day with people they did not play bridge with, buy another TV, or help meet rising expenses. Some firmly believed their job was at home, and they liked it that way. Others, widowed or divorced, simply had no choice. No one mentioned the women who for years had been combining family and full-time job without fanfare.

Labor statisticians met this trend head-on, rejoicing. More people were needed, they said, to cope with the demands of the growing population. These returners would be a source of supply. They could comprise a large proportion of the 7 million women who would take jobs in the next decade, thus providing the help the nation wanted.

But that was more easily said than done. Helping hands must be skilled. The returner is skilled in running a house, educating children, serving on committees, conducting meetings, but not in the latest requirements of the job world.

Returners are eager to go to work, usually know what they want in the long run, are dependable, will stay. Employers are ready to hire them. Yet each group has strings attached. You can plan your return more easily if you understand both sets of strings.

THE STRINGS ATTACHED TO THE RETURNER:

—A woman with family responsibilities has limited hours at her disposal; therefore the job usually must be *part-time.*

—Her husband may want her to be free for winter trips; that means she may seek frequent vacations as well as long summer ones with her children.

—Her interests are more defined now; she may want to make a fresh start and not use past skills and experience.

—She has gone beyond the beginning stage in her life; she is looking for something at an experienced level.

—Sometimes money is not her motive; this makes her more particular about what she will accept, and hence it may take her longer to find it.

—Having attained a respected position at home and in the community, she is at the top of her bailiwick, analogous to a senior at the peak of her educational career; it is discouraging to her to find she can't always get a job commensurate with these achievements.

THE EMPLOYER'S ATTITUDE:

—He wants an employee there all day, and on a regular schedule—for continuity, and effect on customers and other employees.

—He finds that the part-timer, coming in late, is not understood by the full-time staff straining to arrive early.

—Or he finds returners out of practice in conforming to a nine-to-five discipline, routine, deadlines.

—He questions the value of volunteer work as a job recommendation because people can take it or leave it, change hours, get substitutes—a behavior pattern not helpful in a paying job.

—He cannot assign a responsible job to someone who is unfamiliar with the company and the ways of its business—especially when her paid experience is rusty.

SHOULD YOU GO BACK TO WORK? Think about it before you start looking into jobs. Consider your husband and children. Are they ready for it, willing to be deprived of whatever they have to be deprived of? Your husband may have to put things on the stove when you're late, or help with the dishes if you have a meeting; children should be old enough not to feel neglected, not to resent having someone else nurse their colds. Can you find a reliable someone else? All this must be thought out, discussed, agreed upon.

What is the income tax situation? Will your additional salary put the family into a higher bracket? Will you have to pay a baby-sitter more than you will earn at first? Have you allowed for lunches out, carfare, extra clothes, wear and tear on them, wear and tear on *you?* One study showed that half the income of working wives went to expenses connected with their work.

Are you in good health? You must be, and continually. You are taking on not just a job, but *another* job.

Why do you want to go to work? The reason should be positive: for income or training; not negative: to get away from something; or vague: to organize your life. Have you time to devote to it? Will you do whatever you must to get it?

PROVE YOUR VALUE. It is up to you to point out where you could be useful. Size up your background, interests, and aims.

Make a résumé. Explore the market just as you did when you graduated. Go along with the normal processes of looking for a job, fill out applications completely, follow suggestions.

Include your volunteer work, but don't separate it from paid experience and label it. You *did* it; that's what counts, paid or not. Be specific. Instead of just saying modestly that you were chairman of the PTA newsletter committee, you might say you planned weekly newsletters, assigned articles, rewrote and copy-edited them, designed the layout, and saw the finished copy through to the printer. Then relate this work to your aim.

Mrs. R wanted a job when her children went to college. It was 20 years since she had had a salary, but meanwhile she had worked with the Girl Scouts, hospital auxiliary, League of Women Voters. She read a blind ad that called for an executive in a women's organization. She answered it with a letter that described her speaking at women's fund-raising committees, scheduling volunteers, drafting appeals for a white elephant sale. Because her experience was closely related to the work of the organization, and she emphasized what was pertinent, she got an interview, gave a good account of herself, and landed the job.

When you find out what the opportunities are in your area, be willing to take progressive steps toward your final goal, instead of trying to jump over intervening ones. If you need secretarial skills to get you going, brush up the ones you have, or else acquire them. Mrs. F's goal was remedial work, but she knew she was out of practice. She agreed to look for a secretarial job, and in consequence was able to find one in a school only a block from home. In two years she became a member of the remedial reading department.

Beginning in a volunteer capacity to prove what you can do may start you off. Mrs. B spent a year and a half trying to persuade international organizations to hire her as a public relations assistant, and yet she had no tangible evidence of her ability other than a foreign language and an avowed flair for writing. She talked only in vague generalities and convinced no one. Finally she volunteered for an organization that was setting up a refugee section, and quickly turned her words into actions: she met planes at odd hours, produced news releases needed in a hurry, escorted groups of international visitors on sight-seeing trips. Two months later she was on the payroll.

Be overconscientious about duties and hours on the job. One returner endeared herself to the full-time employees in her office by telling them they made her feel guilty when she left early and they were still working.

SOME JOB POSSIBILITIES. In the professions, those with pertinent degrees and past experience can step back into library work, nursing, occupational and physical therapy, social work, and teaching. Psychologists and vocational counselors are scarce in some parts of the country, abundant in others. If you are thinking of embarking on a profession for the first time, learn first what the local situation is and the attitude of the graduate schools you are considering. Age may stand in your way in school even when it does not on the job.

Scientists may have difficulty getting placed because of advances made since they graduated. But some universities hire scientists with a bachelor's degree for training in programming on a part-time or full-time basis. Mathematicians who have had data-processing experience can return to this work in industry.

As for business, those who have had insurance training may re-enter this field and continue their careers after catching up. People with energy and an interest in competition are wanted by the retail field. Part-time sales jobs are plentiful in stores.

Give some thought to starting your own business, especially if you have several talents and are finding the regimen of job hunting difficult. Canvass your neighborhood; see what the lacks are. The free-lance area is one to explore if your experience is in condition.

Selling real estate, insurance, and mutual funds are areas where you can set your own hours and vacations, and develop the job as far as you want.

If you want part-time work, your best bet is to start full time—and after you have proven your ability, ask for shorter hours.

On the whole, good fields for part-time work are:

—secretarial work—which can lead anywhere;
—market research—a natural for continual assignments;
—beauty services—as a job or your own business;
—teaching or office work in schools—which provide both a steady salary and hours to fit your children's;
—fund-raising—provided you are experienced.

There is no single answer for all returners, and few of them have duplicated what others have done. Each must analyze her own situation and the current market, and tailor her actions to fit them.

XXV

CHANGING JOBS

If you don't have to change jobs, don't. The analogy of the rolling stone is still good, in spite of the retort about who wants to gather moss. Try not to leave one job until you have another; and don't change until you can list at least two things you are positive will be better in the next.

If you think you want to leave, be sure you mean it. If the present staff seems hard to get along with, the salary unsatisfactory, working conditions uncomfortable, remember that you risk replacing this set of inconveniences with another. Employment agencies often interview someone in the morning from Company A, wanting to work for Company B; and in the afternoon, one from B wanting A: both applicants convinced that a shift will be an improvement.

If you do have to make a change, it will be easier if you observe the ground rules which are guided by the reason for the change.

THE DISCOURAGED BEGINNER. "I am getting nowhere. I have been doing clerical work for a month; therefore, I want to leave," is a familiar and often illogical statement of a recent graduate.

Everyone realizes you need a job to know a job. You are allowed to make a mistake in selecting your first job, or even your second. But be sure not to consider training immobility.

All jobs, even presidencies, have their routine. You had mundane tasks in college (making lists of books before you could read them, learning formulas before you could apply them, studying complex concepts before you could incorporate them).

Beginning clerical jobs are apprenticeships. So learn all you can before moving away. Have a talk with your supervisor or the personnel department. Find out what lies ahead. And make sure you understand the context of your present work. A thing can be made interesting if given meaning. Adelaide O got a job with a public relations firm. For days she folded letters, put them into envelopes with enclosures, sealed and stamped them. She thought the work was futile. Then her boss told her he hoped to raise several hundred dollars for an international welfare agency through that mailing, and she found herself sparked to finish soon to see the results.

If you *do* find you have made the wrong choice of job, admit it early and leave. It is costing your employer money, and you time. Some companies spend thousands of dollars to train an employee.

Think carefully about what you disliked, what you do want, and then reopen the lines you had out before, but be aware that you are starting anew and probably cannot have credit for brief job experience.

NO PLACE TO GO. The person who has worked her way up and to the top of her department and who has no future ahead may find she can move to a larger company and up a rung, or that she must drop back a bit and begin over. Supply and demand determine which. Sometimes she is between two stools, with too little experience for some openings, too much for others. For instance, Yvonne P had been with an encyclopedia for four years and was in charge of writing and editing the art and archaeology entries. A transfer to another section meant discarding her training. It took her a year to find another job: it was not as good as what she had left, and it meant a cut in salary, but it had room for advancement.

The crucial point is that although you take with you whatever experience you have had, you still must master the ways of another employer. A bus driver is paid for his driving skill *and* for his knowledge of the routes; he is not equipped to operate a bus for another line until he learns its roads. Your value grows with your increased knowledge of the *company*, not just of the *job*.

Often persistence does the trick. Dora W wanted to do research for a certain news commentator, and so she joined the secretarial pool at his network. Every six months she became discouraged and thought of leaving, but each time she was persuaded to hold out. Three years later, the day after her last persuasion, she got the job she wanted.

LAID OFF OR FIRED.   Call a spade a spade. It is no disgrace to be asked to leave a job, and it has happened to the best people. Some years ago a girl was fired from her first job because her lisp prevented her from doing telephone work; today she is a college president. If it happens to you, say so. Your references will disclose it anyway; and you can't have a relaxed interview if you are not honest from the start. Important too: speak kindly of your employer. It does not help you get a job if you let rancor show; it reflects on your manners, and makes the next employer wonder how you will talk about him.

Looking for a job is a sensitive situation at best. If the reason for looking embarrasses you, then it becomes more sensitive. Friends feel concerned, but no way has been found for them to phrase an inquiry tactfully. Get there first by telling them about your progress. Instead of having to answer that you haven't found a job yet, make a decisive statement about what you *are* doing. For instance, you have a number of irons in the fire, things pending, several interviews were encouraging, you are considering an offer, are getting special preparation, or have taken a temporary job until your plans are definite. What you say is less important than how you say it; just sound sure.

CHANGING FROM GOVERNMENT TO PRIVATE INDUSTRY? People who leave a government agency or armed service sometimes make two mistakes. They talk in governmentese; they insist their work was confidential and cannot be described. Semantics are often the answer.

WAVEs or Wacs should make résumés that discuss work in everyday language, omitting ranks and terms like "enlisted personnel," "active duty," "liberty" and "leave," "logistic mobilization plans," "post exchange"—all of which can be translated to give the same information for any setting.

Those who did confidential work can go into detail about what they *did* (which is all anybody wants to know anyway), without ever mentioning the subject matter. You can discuss how you edited reports, made speeches, wrote descriptions, interviewed applicants. None of that divulges anything top secret but it does tell about you.

FROM TEACHING TO NON-TEACHING? Employers sometimes think teachers are too specialized to handle other kinds of work. Bethia D taught modern dance for 16 years in a school in Los Angeles. Then she decided she wanted to try her hand at business. She had an outgoing nature that was immediately apparent to those who interviewed her, and a businesslike attitude in her handling of questions put to her. A department store hired her and she began behind a counter. Her teaching discipline made her conscientious about learning details and keeping records; her dance background taught her the meaning of teamwork; and her experience with people enabled her to work with customers and buyers. In seven months she was promoted to section manager and was on her way to a new career.

FROM VOLUNTEER TO PAID WORK? The returner is actually a person changing fields. We have already discussed methods for her to use. Let us consider here some of the thinking that she might do about *not* taking a paid job.

If her motive is to get away from volunteer work because: the organization is inefficient; she has gone as far as she can; the only work she is given is clerical; rising professional standards make it hard for her to hold her own; the work does not seem worthwhile—all reasons frequently cited—then she might first see if she could alter the situation. The way our society is set up, much of the work necessary for survival cannot finance itself. Social welfare offices, health agencies, medical research, adoption groups must have voluntary support and help. Meeting illness, personal tragedy, disaster, and charging for it are mutually exclusive. We cannot afford to lose volunteers.

Take a look at the agency you are working for. If it is disorganized, could you make it less so? If you feel at a dead end, perhaps initiative could open up new areas (the same thing happens in salaried jobs). If you are not given absorbing work to do, perhaps your display of lack of interest hides your potentialities. If you find the professional staff in your way, try another agency. Mrs. H, a librarian, does volunteer library work for her son's school; Mrs. L, a psychologist, contributes her testing services to a counseling office. If you think your dinner guest's day planning a press party sounds more important than yours running a camp for handicapped children, perhaps it is because she talks more convincingly.

TOP LEVEL CHANGE? Some women want to change because they finally admit, after many years, that they never liked their subject. They must give such a decision a lot of thought, because the more specialized and experienced they are, the harder it will be for them.

Employers are sometimes slow to see the possibility of applying techniques. As one wag put it, an advertising agency looking for a copywriter for a dry-cereal account may turn down those with cooked-cereal experience. A professional organization may be afraid of someone with a commercial background.

The clue is in the way you express it, and the change can be made if skills rather than subject matter or fields are stressed. Mrs. T, a fashion writer, wanted to enter the non-profit field. She applied to welfare agencies for a public relations job, but could not convince them that she could talk their language when she outlined her fashion know-how. So she drafted a résumé that pointed up her writing of news releases and promotion pieces without stressing the subject, and she described her volunteer work with fund-raising committees. Result: she was appointed public relations director for a settlement house.

Sometimes complete retraining toward a job that is hard to fill is the answer. Patricia W spent 15 years with a mail-order house and had become a buyer. But she was giving most of her life to the job; she worked until nine o'clock many nights, and sometimes a large part of the weekends. Although she loved the work, she felt she wanted more of a life of her own. Yet her specialized training meant that she could continue to command that salary only in similar work. She saw that the solution was to train herself for a shortage area. She went to secretarial school, learned shorthand and typing, and got a job as secretary to the president of an industrial concern. Her business knowledge and judgment of people were put to use as soon as she learned the business, and within a year she was earning as much as she would have been in her former job.

AFTER RETIREMENT?   Sixty-five is young today, and many who retire then want to continue to work. Sometimes they have to. Some want a full-time job, others only a part-time one to add to their social security. Against them are their years (they probably won't work another decade) and the fact that part-time jobs are comparatively scarce.

Such older applicants need to prove that they are not rigid

but can follow new directions. Inflexibility is not necessarily a characteristic of age, but if it occurs it can cost a job. Mrs. G was a good typist and she got a job as an office assistant with an insurance company after retirement. She was taught to use an addressograph machine, but resisted it, and although she listened to the directions, she determined to use her own way. The next time a set of envelopes had to be run off, her boss saw her sitting at a typewriter addressing each envelope individually, reading from the plates. Her unwillingness to accept new methods lost her the job.

In a large city it is best to hand-pick the places to approach. On the whole, smaller companies and non-profit organizations are the best prospects. They are less likely to have personnel policies that preclude taking retired people; and they may have small budgets that cannot afford all the full-time skills they need.

Miss S was a librarian. When she retired she needed to keep on earning some money, and so she looked for a part-time job. Although she never found a permanent one, what she did find added up to more than she needed. In one instance she was called on to catalogue a private collection; in another she substituted for a librarian on vacation; once she ran a reprint department. In every case she applied only for what she was qualified to do.

Bookkeepers are called back by former employers to help during peak seasons. Publishers hire teachers to advise their high school textbook departments; universities with a higher retirement age take on retired professors. Foundations sometimes engage the retired to direct short-term studies. Insurance companies, mutual funds, and the real estate field beckon because experience means contacts which are useful to them.

The problem may be more in *finding* the job than in *getting* it.

GEOGRAPHIC CHANGE? Moving from one part of the country

to another can present difficulties, sometimes insurmountable, but that need not mean failure. Eileen C was the editor of a trade journal in Indiana. She was completely responsible for getting out the publication. Thinking a similar job in New York would be bigger and better, she took time off to explore, visited many publications, talked to employment agencies, and found it would take months for her to get anything like what she had, and even then it would not have as much scope. She realized she was better off than she thought, and she went home satisfied to stay.

If a geographic change must be made for personal reasons, such as a husband's transfer, than follow the basic job-hunting techniques, be on the spot for interviews, and accept the fact that what you want may take a while to find.

FINALE

It is a feminine characteristic to continue shopping for something even after we have found just what we want. But beware of that other side of the fence. A job is not a commodity we pick off a shelf, use, then discard for another. It is something that becomes part of us, grows with us.

It is up to you to make the grass greener on your side, and you can.

PUBLICATIONS MENTIONED IN THIS BOOK

Civil Service Leader. Published weekly.

Dictionary of Occupational Titles. Washington: U.S. Government Printing Office, 1949.

EISENBERG, SALLY. *How to Earn an Income Selling Products and Services by Phone.* Greenlawn, N.Y.: Harian Publications, 1952.

FORRESTER, GERTRUDE. *Occupational Literature, An Annotated Bibliography.* New York: H. W. Wilson Co., 1958.

Literary Market Place. New York: R. R. Bowker Co. Published yearly.

McKittrick Directory of Advertisers. New York: George McKittrick & Co. Published yearly.

MELCHER, DANIEL. *So You Want to Get into Book Publishing.* New York: R. R. Bowker Co., 1962.

Occupational Outlook Handbook. Washington: U.S. Government Printing Office, 1961.

Printers' Ink Directory of House Organs. New York: Printers' Ink Publishing Co., 1954.

Publishers' Weekly. New York: R. R. Bowker Co. Published weekly.

REDGRAVE, WILLIAM. *Why Not Write.* Greenlawn, N.Y.: Harian Publications, 1956.

Ross Reports Talent Edition. New York: Television Index, Inc. Published monthly.

Small Business Administration. Washington 25, D.C. Publishes bulletins and releases on all kinds and most phases of business.

The Standard Advertising Register. New York: National Register Publishing Co. Published yearly.

Thomas' Register of American Manufacturers. New York: Thomas Publishing Co. Published yearly.

U.S. Department of Labor, Women's Bureau. Washington 25, D.C. Publishes materials concerning women's employment.

U.S. Government Printing Office, Division of Public Documents. Washington 25, D.C. Publishes materials on many subjects.

Variety. Published weekly.

ACKNOWLEDGMENTS

Many hands made this book. The volumes I have consulted in 20 years of placement work are too numerous to list, and I must acknowledge them anonymously. Some, of perennial help, are referred to in the text.

Yeoman service has been rendered by those who have read and commented on individual chapters. My role in maintaining the balance of loyalty to job hunters and the businesses who seek them has been a tightrope-walking operation. For every action there is an equal and opposite reaction. The final responsibility is mine, but grateful thanks are due to: Mr. Kermit J. Berylson—Rosen, Futerman and Berylson; Mrs. Ingeborg Bondi—Editor, Magnum Photos, Inc.; Mr. Jean Boutyette—Staff Executive, American Association of Advertising Agencies; Mr. Amory H. Bradford—Vice President and General Manager, *The New York Times;* Mr. Vincent P. Brennan—Vice President, Bloomingdale's; Mr. Ralph F. Chipchase—Employment Manager, American Express Company; Mr. David M. Church—former Executive Director, American Association of Fund-Raising Counsel, Inc.; Miss Ruth Davenport—Owner, Abilities Located; Mrs. Kenneth Dorland—Real Estate Saleswoman; Mr. Milton Glaser—Milton Glaser Associates, and President, American Institute of Interior Designers; Mrs. Russell K. Jones—Vice President, Fiduciary Trust Company of New York; Mrs. Alice K. Leopold—former Assistant to the Secretary of Labor and Director of the Women's Bureau of the Department of Labor; Miss Betty S. Martin—Director, Women's Division, Institute of Life Insurance; Mr. Harold Oberg —Director of Research, National Association of Investment

Companies; Mr. Harry Paster—Staff Executive, American Association of Advertising Agencies; Mr. Ralph M. Payne—Public Information Supervisor, American Telephone and Telegraph Company; Mr. Elmo Roper—Elmo Roper Associates; Mr. Norman G. Shidle—Editor, *SAE Journal;* Miss Helen Taft—District Education Manager, International Business Machines Corporation; Mrs. Sara N. Thompson—Administrative Associate, The Center for Programmed Instruction, Inc.; Mrs. Howard B. Tingue—Fiction Editor, *McCall's;* Miss Mary Walker—Taylor-Walker Associates, and Chairman, National Public Relations Committee, American Women in Radio and Television; Miss Louise Watson —R. W. Pressprich and Company.

A wealthy source of data was the New York Public Library books and vertical file materials. The New York Society Library, besides supplying books, checked references and smoked out information quickly and thoroughly.

Rare support has come from Marion King, mother, librarian, author, whose patient rereadings, careful suggestions, and steady typing have made molehills out of mountains.

INDEX

account executive, advertising, 46

accounting, 65-69, 98; certified public accountant (CPA), 66

acting, 39, 168

actuary, 110

advertising, 40-49; research, 40-41; media, 41; copywriting, 42, 74; publicity, 43; production, 44; account executive, 46; telephone solicitor, 160

Agriculture, Department of, 99

airline, 183-86; stewardess, 183; reservation agent, 185

announcer, radio and television, 168

application form, 7-9

archaeology, 33, 101

architecture, 33, 101; landscape, 33

Armed Services, 50-56; Personnel, 52; Special Services, 53; Information, 54; Communications, 54; Intelligence, 54; Logistics, 54; Finance, 55; Air Operations Support, 55; Food Services, 55

art, jobs with, 33, 43, 46, 55, 71, 72, 92, 102, 143, 153, 157, 161, 169

astronomer, 101

auditing, 66, 112

automation, 57-63, 98; computer or systems analyst, 58; programmer, 58; systems engineer or representative, 60; card punch machine operator, 62; verifying operator, 62; console operator, 62; computer operator, 62; tape librarian, 62

bacteriologist, 101

banking, 82-85; bank teller, 82; bank clerk, 82-83; non-banking jobs in, 83; investment, 87-88

biology, 33, 101

bookkeeping, 64-65, 98

book publishing, 149-56; reader, 149; editing, 149-50, 152; proofreading, 151-52; production, 153, 157; subsidiary rights, 154; promotion, 154; publicity, 154; sales, 155; literary agent, 163; free-lance jobs, 164

broker, stock, 87; insurance, 107; real estate, 178

brokerage, 85-87; clerk, 85; junior analyst, 86; registered representative, 87; security analyst, 87; portfolio analyst, 87

buyer, 72-73

card punch machine operator, 62
cartographer, 101
changing jobs, 195
chartist, 122
chemistry, 33, 101
city planning, 33
Civil Service Commission, 96
clerical jobs, 24-31
coder, 122, 142
colorist, 71
Commerce, Department of, 99
comparison shopper, 74
computer, 58; analyst, 58; operator, 62
console operator, 62
copy testing, 120
copywriter, 42, 74-75, 111
correspondent, 111, 142, 157, 160
cub reporter, 159
curator, museum, 102

dance, 34
data processing, 58
decorator, 99, 118
dental hygienist, 34, 102; technician, 34
design, interior, 99, 114-18
designer, fashion, 72
dietician, 102
disc jockey, 172
docent, museum, 102

economist, 47
editing, 74, 99-100, 112, 123, 142, 151-52, 156, 161; editor, accessories, 74; fashion, 74; special, 152, 156, 161; copy, 151; editorial assistant, 142, 157
educational requirements for jobs; *see* specific job categories

employment agencies, how to use, 7-8; jobs with, 132
engineer, 47; systems, 60
entomologist, 102
executive recruiting, 135-36

fashion, 70-75; advertising, 46, 74; apprentice, 71; colorist, 71; model, 71-72; buyer, 72-73; designer, 72, 74; coordinator, 73-74; editor, 74; photographer, 74; *see also* retailing
Federal Communications Commission (FCC), 100
Federal Housing Administration, 98
Federal Service Entrance Examination (FSSE), 97
filing, clerk, 25; supervisor, 25
finance, 55, 81-89, 98; banking, 82-85; brokerage, 85-87; investment counseling, 88; mutual funds, 88-89
free-lance, 90-95
fund-raising, 144-47

General Accounting Office, 98
geology, 34, 102
geophysicist, 102
Girl Friday; *see* secretary
government, 96-104, 186; changing from government to private industry, 198
Government Printing Office, 100

Health, Education, and Welfare, Department of, 99
home economics, 34, 55, 102

Housing and Home Finance Agency, 101

illustrator, 102
insurance, 98, 105-13; claims examiner, 99; adjuster, 108; life insurance underwriter, 107; branch manager, 107; agent, 107; broker, 107; saleswoman, 107; underwriter, 109; actuary, 110; correspondent, 111; policy form drafter, 111; non-insurance jobs in, 111
interior design, 99, 114-18; decorator, 99, 118
Internal Revenue Service, 98
International Broadcasting Service, 101
International Motion Picture Service, 101
interview, job, 15
interviewer, 120, 127, 133-34, 142; market research, 120; employment, 127; placement, 133-34; research, 142
investment, 85-88, 111; brokerage, 85-87; banking, 87-88; counseling, 88; in insurance, 111

Job Finding Forum of the Advertising Club, 14
job-hunt, how to, 7-23
jobs or training, further information about; *see* end of specific job chapters

Labor, Department of, 99; Women's Bureau, 99
laboratory assistant, 33, 37

law, 35, 47, 56, 102, 111; legal file clerk, 35
layout, 43-45
letter of application, 15
library, 35, 122, 170; special, 35; music, 170; librarian, 62, 102-103, 122, 161; tape, 62; medical record, 103
Library of Congress, 103
literary agent, 163

magazine publishing, 156-59; special editor, 156; editorial assistant, 157; correspondent, 157; production, 157; sales, 158; literary agent, 163; free-lance jobs, 164
management consultant, 135
Man Marketing Clinic, 14
market research, 99, 119-25; interviewer, 120-21; statistician, 121; coder, 122; tabulator, 122; chartist, 122
media, advertising, 41; testing, 120
medicine, 35, 111; medical technician, 35; medical record librarian, 103
merchandising, 76; section manager, 76; stock clerk, 76; head of stock, 76; *see also* retailing
model, 71-72
motivation research, 120
museum, 33; curator, 102; docent, 102
music, 36, 56, 170
mutual funds, 88-89

National Advisory Committee on Aeronautics, 98

National Archives and Records Service, 100

newspaper publishing, 159-63; cub reporter, 159; copy girl, 159; reporter, 160; stringer, 160; columnist, 160; correspondent, 160; copyreader, 160; editorial clerk, 160; advertising telephone solicitor, 160; special editor, 161; circulation, 162; free-lance jobs, 164-65

notary public, 93

numbers, jobs with, 40, 54-55, 64-69, 109, 156

nursing, 36, 103, 111; nurse's aide, 36; practical nurse, 37

occupational therapist, 36

office services, temporary, 30

own business, 91

part time, 190-91, 194

people, jobs with, 24, 52-53, 106, 120, 126-36, 143, 183

personnel, 52, 76, 99, 126-32; employment interviewer, 127; counseling, 128; safety administration, 128; labor relations, 130; wage and salary administration, 130; job analysis and evaluation, 131

photographer, 74, 137-39, 143

physical therapist, 37

physics, 37, 103

physiologist, 103

picture stylist, 74

placement, 132-35

portfolio analyst, 87

production, 44, 153, 157, 171; advertising, 44; publishing, 153,

157; radio, 171

professions, non-professional jobs within, 32-39

programmed instruction, 152-53

programmer, 58-60, 112; trainee, 58, 60

promotion, 77, 154, 160; sales, 77; publishing, 154; writer, 160

proofreader, 151-52

psychology, 37, 47, 103

psychometrist, 37

publications mentioned in this book, 203

publicity, 43, 154, 169; advertising, 43; publishing, 154; radio, 169

public relations, 99, 112, 140-44, 162

publishing, 100, 148-63; book, 149-56; magazine, 156-59; newspaper, 159-63

puppeteering, 39

radio, 46-47, 100, 167-75; announcer, 168; weather girl, 168; writing, 169-70; production assistant, 171; program director, 171; disc jockey, 172; program coordinator, 172; production coordinator, 172

Railroad Retirement Board, 98

real estate, 101, 176-78; agent, 176; saleswoman, 176; rental agent, 177; broker, 178

receptionist, 24; receptionist-interviewer, 127

recreation, 37, 103

registered representative, 87

religion, 38

reporter, 159

research, jobs with, 151, 158, 171;

advertising, 40-41; media, 41; finance, 87; market, 99; consumer, 119; motivation, 120; public opinion, 120; interviewer, 120, 142; public relations, 120, 142-43; personnel, 130

résumé, 10-14; samples, 11-13; how to list volunteer work, 192; for those changing fields, 198, 200

retailing, 70-80; sales clerk, 71; comparison shopper, 74; merchandising, 76; personnel, 76; sales promotion, 77; financial control, 77; store operations, 77; *see also* fashion

retired, 200

returner, 189-94; her requirements, 190; employers' requirements, 190-91; job possibilities, 193-94

salary, withholdings, 20; *see also* specific job categories

sales, 71, 77, 107, 119, 173, 176; fashion, 71; promotion, 77; insurance, 107; testing, 119; radio and television, 173; real estate, 176

scientist, jobs for, 33, 35, 37, 55, 101-103

secretary, 27-30; other titles, 29; jobs that call for, 28; administrative or executive, 30

section manager, 76

Securities and Exchange Commission, 98

security analyst, 87

Small Business Administration, 98

Social Security Administration, 99

social work, 38, 103; investigator, 38; group work, 38; case aide, 38

State Employment Services, 7, 97, 99

statistician, 87, 121

stenographer, 27

stewardess, airline, 183

stringer, 160

stylist, 72, 74

systems analyst, 58; systems engineer, 60; systems representative, 60

tabulator, 122, 142

teacher, 38, 104, 128

technician, dental, 34; medical, 35

telephone, 179-81; advertising solicitor, 160; operator, 179; service representative, 180

television, 46-47, 167-75; weather girl, 168; announcer, 168; writing, 169-70; production assistant, 171

teller, bank, 82

temporary office services, 30

theatre, 39

travel, 182-88; airlines, 183-86; airline stewardess, 183; airline reservation agent, 185; agency, 186; government work, 186; representative, 187

typist, 26

underwriter, 107, 109

United States Information Agency, 101

Urban Renewal Administration, 101

verifying operator, 62

Veterans' Administration, 98
Voice of America; *see* International Broadcasting Service
volunteer work, 146, 198

wages; *see* salary
weather girl, 168

where the jobs are; *see* specific job categories
Women's Bureau of the Department of Labor, 99
writing, jobs with, 42-43, 54, 74-75, 99-100, 111, 131, 142, 154-55, 160, 169-70; copywriting, 42, 155; promotion, 160